D0427560

GOD'S DAILY
INSIGHTS™
FOR *Women*

HARVEST HOUSE PUBLISHERS
EUGENE, OREGON

Scripture versions used are listed on page 175.

Cover design by Garborg Design Works

Interior design by KUHN Design Group

Editorial development by Meadow's Edge Group LLC

For bulk, special sales, or ministry purchases, please call 1 (800) 547-8979.
Email: Customerservice@hhpbooks.com

ꟿ is a federally registered trademark of the Hawkins Children's LLC. Harvest House Publishers, Inc., is the exclusive licensee of the trademark.

GOD'S DAILY INSIGHTS is a trademark of The Hawkins Children's LLC. Harvest House Publishers, Inc., is the exclusive licensee of the trademark GOD'S DAILY INSIGHTS.

God's Daily Insights™ for Women

Copyright © 2022 by Meadow's Edge Group LLC
Published by Harvest House Publishers
Eugene, Oregon 97408
www.harvesthousepublishers.com

ISBN 978-0-7369-8129-3 (Milano Softone®)
ISBN 978-0-7369-8130-9 (eBook)

Library of Congress Control Number: 2021943515

Printed in China

21 22 23 24 25 26 27 28 29 / RDS / 10 9 8 7 6 5 4 3 2 1

INTRODUCTION

Each day in our lives is a journey, and the path we walk is never the same—at least it feels that way most days. Each morning, our best intention is to live each day receiving from God the direction, encouragement, hope, and confidence only He can provide.

Seeking God's guidance, discovering His plan, and living it out is a process we can nurture daily. These practices help us grow personally, and they provide inspiration and encouragement we can share with the people around us.

May the words, quotes, and Scriptures in the following pages provide the hope you need. More importantly, may you encounter God along the way.

YOUR DAILY
TIME WITH GOD

Each new day is a gift from God, and if we are wise, we spend a few quiet moments each day in devotion and thanking the Giver. Daily life is woven together with the threads of habit, and no habit is more important to our spiritual health than the discipline of daily prayer and devotion to God.

When we begin each day with God, heads bowed and hearts lifted, we remind ourselves of His love, His protection, and His commandments. And if we are wise, we align our priorities for the coming day with the teachings and commandments God has given us through His Scriptures.

Are you seeking to change some aspect of your life? Would you like to improve your spiritual or physical health? If so, ask for God's help. And ask for it many times each day…starting with your morning devotional.

He awakens Me morning by morning,
He awakens My ear to hear as the learned.
The Lord God has opened My ear.

ISAIAH 50:4-5

GENEROUS GIVING

Do you want to improve your self-esteem? Being generous is a great first step. When you give generously to people who need your help, God will bless your endeavors and enrich your life. So if you're looking for a surefire way to improve the quality of your day or your life, here it is: Find ways to share your blessings.

God rewards generously just as surely as He disciplines us. If we become generous disciples as we serve our Lord, God will bless us in ways we cannot fully understand. But if we allow ourselves to become closed-minded and closefisted—either with our possessions or with our love—we deprive ourselves of the spiritual abundance that could be ours.

Do you seek God's abundance and His peace? Then share the blessings He has given you. Share your possessions, share your faith, share your story, and share your love. God will delight in your generosity—and your neighbors will too.

Each person should do as he has decided in
his heart—not reluctantly or out of compulsion,
since God loves a cheerful giver.

2 CORINTHIANS 9:7 CSB

WHAT IS OUR PERSPECTIVE?

If a temporary loss of perspective has left you worried, exhausted, or both, it's time to readjust your thought patterns. Negative thoughts are habit forming. Thankfully, so are positive ones. With practice, you can form the habit of focusing on God's priorities and your own possibilities. When you do, you'll soon discover you will spend less time fretting about your challenges and more time focusing on God's blessings and praising Him for His gifts.

When you call upon the Lord and prayerfully seek His will, He will give you wisdom and perspective. When you make God's priorities your priorities, He will direct your steps and calm your fears.

So ask God for a sense of balance and perspective. And remember, no problems are too big for Him—including yours.

All I'm doing right now, friends, is showing how these things pertain to Apollos and me so that you will learn restraint and not rush into making judgments without knowing all the facts. It's important to look at things from God's point of view. I would rather not see you inflating or deflating reputations based on mere hearsay.

1 Corinthians 4:6 msg

THE POWER AND
PROMISE OF WISDOM

Where will you find wisdom today? Will you seek it from God or from the world? As a thoughtful woman living in a society that is filled with temptations and distractions, you know the world's brand of "wisdom" is everywhere—and it is dangerous. You live in a world where it's all too easy to stray far from the ultimate source of wisdom: God and His holy Word.

When you commit yourself to getting to know God more through His Word and following His ways—you will become wise…in time. God will bring the growth as you seek His heart.

As a way of understanding God and His plan for your life, study His Word and learn how to live. When you do, you will accumulate a storehouse of wisdom that will enrich your life and the lives of your family members, your friends, and the world around you.

If any of you lacks wisdom, he should ask God—
who gives to all generously and ungrudgingly—
and it will be given to him. But let him ask in
faith without doubting. For the doubter is like
the surging sea, driven and tossed by the wind.

JAMES 1:5-6 CSB

PERSEVERANCE
FOR STRENGTH AND
SUSTAINABILITY

A well-lived life is like a marathon, not a sprint—it calls for preparation, determination, and of course, lots of perseverance. For an example of perfect perseverance, we need look no further than our Savior, Jesus Christ.

Jesus finished what He began. Despite His suffering and the shame of the cross, Jesus was steadfast in His faithfulness to God. He trusted His Father's heart. We too must remain faithful, especially during hard times. Sometimes, God may answer our prayers with silence, and when He does, we must patiently hold His hand and trust His heart.

Are you facing a tough situation? Involved in challenging circumstances? If so, remember this: Whatever you're facing, God can handle it. Your job is to keep trusting Him and keep pressing on until He does.

Thanks be to God, who gives us the victory through
our Lord Jesus Christ. Therefore, my beloved brethren, be
steadfast, immovable, always abounding in the work of the
Lord, knowing that your labor is not in vain in the Lord.

1 CORINTHIANS 15:57-58

THE ESSENTIAL
OF PRAYER

On his second missionary journey, Paul started a small church in Thessalonica. A short time later, he penned a letter to encourage new believers at that church. Today, 1 Thessalonians remains a powerful, practical guide for Christian living.

In the letter, Paul advised members of the new church to "pray without ceasing" (5:17 KJV). His advice applies to Christians of every generation. When we consult God regularly, we receive His wisdom, His strength, and His love. As Corrie ten Boom observed, "Any concern that is too small to be turned into a prayer is too small to be made into a burden."

Today, instead of turning things over in your mind, turn them over to God in prayer. Instead of worrying about your next decision, ask God to lead the way. Don't limit your prayers to meals or bedtime. Become a woman of constant prayer. God is listening, and He delights to hear from you.

Rejoice in hope; be patient in affliction;
be persistent in prayer.

ROMANS 12:12 CSB

HIS SACRIFICE
AND HIS GRACE

Let's take a moment to consider this amazing paradox: Jesus Christ—the King of kings and Lord of lords—lived among us as a humble servant. He was born in obscurity, He ministered mostly in small Galilean towns, and He seemed most comfortable in the company of "the least of these." And then, in the ultimate act of humility and service, He gave His life as a sacrifice for sin. What kind of King is this?

Jesus is the Son of God, but He wore a crown of thorns. He is the Savior of the world, yet He was put to death on a cross of rough-hewn wood. He reached out His hands to heal the sick and raise the dead, but those same hands were pierced with nails. What incredible love, that the Creator of the universe should take on the form of a servant (Philippians 2:7)! What matchless grace, that He "who had no sin [should become] sin for us, so that in him we might become the righteousness of God" (2 Corinthians 5:21 NIV)! Today, let the mystery and wonder of these simple words take root deep in your heart: "Christ…died for us" (Romans 5:6 NLT).

> *God forbid that I should boast except in the cross*
> *of our Lord Jesus Christ, by whom the world*
> *has been crucified to me, and I to the world.*
>
> GALATIANS 6:14

ANYTHING IS POSSIBLE!

As a little girl, you probably believed some unbelievable things—like the tooth fairy exchanged molars for cash or that Santa shimmied down your chimney on Christmas Eve. What you believed, true or not, influenced your actions. You put your tooth under your pillow and left cookies out for Santa. You believed in what you thought was possible.

Some aspects of God seem unbelievable. But He's no fairy tale. Put the historicity of Jesus and the faithfulness of God's promises to the test. Know what you believe and why.

Then, don't just say you believe in God—act on that belief. Release guilt and regret, believing God has forgiven you. Risk being authentically you, believing God created you for a unique purpose. Reach out to others, believing love is God's highest aim for your life.

If you can believe, all things are possible
to him who believes.

Mark 9:23

GOD ACCEPTS EVERYONE

God accepts us—faults and all. Can we do the same for those around us? It's easy to get off track. A different race, different religious beliefs, even a different style of clothes can lead us to make judgments before we speak to someone or get to know them.

The key is to bypass what you see and focus on what you know. God created each person with great love and care. God accepts each person, even if he or she has not accepted Him. The more you learn to view others through God's love instead of sizing them up with your eyes, the easier it will be to accept them as equals, treat them as friends, and love them as God's precious children.

He chose us in Him before the foundation of the world...
according to the good pleasure of His will,
to the praise of the glory of His grace,
by which He made us accepted in the Beloved.

Ephesians 1:4-6

BLESSED WITH EVERY BLESSING

When you count your blessings, your mind most likely turns to the blessings you can see—a warm place to live, food in the fridge, friends and family to hold you close. But the blessings God showers on you every day go far beyond what you can see or touch.

God's blessings include miracles like the privilege of prayer, a future home in heaven, and the ultimate gift of salvation. Although blessings like these are more than the human mind can understand, they are also easily taken for granted. Take time to give God a heartfelt thank-you note via prayer. Ask Him to help your gratitude grow by making you increasingly aware of every blessing He brings your way.

*Praise be to the God and Father of our Lord
Jesus Christ. In Christ, God has given us every
spiritual blessing in the heavenly world.*

EPHESIANS 1:3 NCV

GOD'S PLANS FOR YOU

God has plans for your life, but He won't force His plans on you. He has given you the ability to make decisions on your own. With that freedom comes the responsibility of living with both the opportunities and the consequences of your choices.

Living in harmony with God's plan for your life includes studying His Word, listening to His instructions, and being watchful for His signs. You will naturally associate with fellow believers who, by their words and actions, encourage your spiritual growth. You will increasingly avoid two terrible temptations: the temptation to sin and the temptation to squander time. And you will listen carefully, even reverently, to the conscience God has placed in your heart.

God has glorious plans for you this day and for your life. As you go about your daily activities, keep your eyes and ears open—as well as your heart. As Scripture reveals, "We know that all things work together for the good of those who love God, who are called according to his purpose" (Romans 8:28 CSB).

Teach me to do your will, for you are my God.
May your gracious Spirit lead me on level ground.

PSALM 143:10 CSB

MIRACLES: GOD'S HAND AT WORK

If you haven't seen any of God's miracles lately, perhaps it's time to try looking for them in a new way. Throughout history, the Creator has intervened in the course of human events in ways that cannot be explained by science or human rationale. And He's still doing so today.

God's miracles are not limited to special occasions, nor are they witnessed by a select few. God is crafting His wonders all around us: the miracle of the birth of a new baby, the miracle of a world renewing itself with every sunrise, the miracle of lives transformed by God's love and grace. Each day, God's handiwork is evident for all to see and experience.

Today, seize the opportunity to inspect God's hand at work. His miracles come in a variety of shapes and sizes, so keep your eyes and heart open to what God is doing right in front of you. You'll be amazed by what you see.

Joni Eareckson Tada reminds us, "Faith means believing in realities that go beyond sense and sight. It is the awareness of unseen divine realities all around you."

You are the God who works wonders;
you revealed your strength among the peoples.

Psalm 77:14 csb

THE GOODNESS OF GOD'S GRACE

God's grace is not earned. To earn God's love and His gift of eternal life would be far beyond the abilities of even the most righteous person. Thankfully, grace is not an earthly reward for righteous behavior. It is a blessed spiritual gift that can be accepted by believers who dedicate themselves to God through Christ. When we accept Christ as our Savior, we are saved by His grace, and our lives are transformed as children of God.

The familiar words of Ephesians 2:8 make God's promise perfectly clear: "It is by grace you have been saved, through faith" (NIV). We are saved not because of our good deeds (works), but because of our faith in Christ.

God's grace is the ultimate gift. Let's praise and thank Him for this incredible blessing, and let's share the good news with all who cross our paths. We return our Father's love by accepting His grace and sharing His message and His love. When we do, we are eternally blessed—and the Father smiles.

Grace to you and peace from God our Father
and the Lord Jesus Christ.

PHILIPPIANS 1:2 CSB

HEARING FROM GOD

Sometimes God speaks loudly and clearly. More often, He speaks in a quiet voice. To listen for His voice, carve out quiet moments each day to pray, study His Word, and sense His direction. These quiet moments are the best times to listen to God.

Quiet yourself so you are able to listen to your conscience. Follow the subtle guidance of your intuition, which God has given you. Pray sincerely and wait quietly for His response. God usually refrains from sending His messages on stone tablets or city billboards, so quieting our hearts is the best way to hear from Him. Let's focus on the subtler ways He communicates. The silent corner of a quiet, willing heart is a wonderful place to encounter your heavenly Father.

The one who is from God listens to God's words.

JOHN 8:47 CSB

THE FEAR OF THE LORD

God's Word teaches that "the fear of the LORD is the beginning of knowledge" (Proverbs 1:7). Are you a woman who possesses a healthy, fearful respect for God's power?

When we fear the Lord and honor Him by obeying His commandments, we receive God's blessings. However, when we ignore Him or disobey His commandments, disastrous consequences result.

God's hand shapes the universe, and it shapes our lives. God maintains absolute sovereignty over His creation, and His power is beyond comprehension. The fear of the Lord is indeed the beginning of knowledge, but thankfully, once we possess a healthy and reverent fear of God, we don't have to fear anything else.

Precept Ministries founder Kay Arthur states it like this: "To know that God rules over all—that there are no accidents in life, that no tactic of Satan or man can ever thwart the will of God—brings divine comfort."

Since we are receiving a kingdom that cannot be shaken,
let us be thankful. By it, we may serve God acceptably,
with reverence and awe.

HEBREWS 12:28 CSB

THOUGHTS OF DOUBT

If you've never had any doubts about your faith, feel free to stop reading this page and skip to the next devotion! However, if you're like the rest of us who know what it's like to struggle with doubts about your faith or your God, keep reading.

Even the most faithful Christians sometimes face discouragement and doubt. But even when we feel far removed from God, He is never far removed from us. He is always with us, always willing to calm the storms of life, and always willing to replace our doubts with His comfort and assurance.

Whenever you're plagued by doubt, go ahead—talk with God about it. Don't worry; He won't be offended. Seek His presence by cultivating a deeper and increasingly honest relationship with His Son. Then rest assured, God will calm your fears, answer your prayers, and restore your confidence.

Because you have seen me, you have believed.
Blessed are those who have not seen and yet believe.

JOHN 20:29 CSB

A SERVANT'S HEART

Jesus taught that the most esteemed men and women were not the self-congratulatory leaders of society but were instead the humblest of servants. But sometimes we fall short— we seek to puff up ourselves and glorify our accomplishments. To do so sets the wrong example as believers.

With the societal pressures we face today, it's easy to fall into a "me trap" of building ourselves up in the eyes of those around us. Instead, let's find ways to serve those in need. Let's volunteer with mission-driven organizations that meet other people's needs. Sometimes it's as easy as lending a helping hand and sharing an act of kindness. This is God's way of serving others.

Humble servants are more interested in following Christ's example than they are in impressing other people. And that's what God intends. After all, earthly glory is fleeting, but heavenly glory endures through eternity.

> Be strong and of good courage, and do it; do not fear nor be
> dismayed, for the LORD God—my God—will be with you.
> He will not leave you nor forsake you, until you have
> finished all the work for the service of the house of the LORD.
>
> 1 CHRONICLES 28:20

OPEN YOUR HEART

In his book *The Four Loves*, C.S. Lewis observed, "Every Christian would agree that a man's spiritual health is exactly proportional to his love for God." We can enjoy the spiritual health God intends for us by praising Him, loving Him, and obeying Him.

When we worship our heavenly Father faithfully and obediently, we invite His love into our hearts. We allow Him to rule over our days and our lives. In turn, we grow to love God even more deeply as we sense His love for us.

Saint Augustine wrote, "I love you, Lord, not doubtingly, but with absolute certainty. Your Word beat upon my heart until I fell in love with you, and now the universe and everything in it tells me to love you."

Today, open your heart to the Father, and let your obedience be a fitting response to His never-ending love.

We know that all things work together
for the good of those who love God,
who are called according to his purpose.

Romans 8:28 csb

BEING A GOOD STEWARD

The gifts you possess are gifts from the Giver of all things good. Do you have a spiritual gift? If so, share it. Do you have a testimony about the things Christ has done for you? If so, don't leave your story untold. Do you possess financial resources? If so, share them. Do you have particular talents? Hone your skills and use them for God's glory.

The best way to discover your spiritual gifts is to simply start doing what you believe God wants you to do. As you serve Him, you will find He has given you gifts that empower you to serve Him.

When we hoard the treasures God has given us, we deprive ourselves and others of blessings and joy. But when we obey God by sharing His gifts freely and without fanfare, we invite Him to bless us more and more. Be a faithful steward of your talents and treasures, and then prepare yourself for even greater blessings that are sure to come.

Just as each one has received a gift, use it to serve others,
as good stewards of the varied grace of God.

1 PETER 4:10 CSB

BE STILL AND LISTEN

We live in a noisy society that creates distractions, frustrations, and complications. If we allow the distractions of a clamorous world to separate us from God's peace, we do ourselves a profound disservice.

If we seek to maintain righteous minds and compassionate hearts, we should take time each day to pray and meditate. We should seek stillness in the presence of the Lord. As we quiet our minds and our hearts, we can listen to the Holy Spirit and sense God's will for our lives.

Many of us battle busy schedules, often rushing through the day without a single moment for quiet contemplation and prayer. If this sounds like you, consider this as an invitation to reconsider your priorities.

Has the busy pace of life robbed you of the peace that could be yours through Jesus Christ? Nothing is more important than time spent with the Savior. So be still and claim the inner peace that is your spiritual birthright: the peace of Jesus Christ.

Be still, and know that I am God.

PSALM 46:10

A BRIGHT FUTURE

How bright is your future? Do you think about what God may have planned for your life? Well, if you're a faithful believer, God's plans for you are so bright, you'd better have your sunglasses nearby. But take a moment to ask yourself this: How bright do you believe your future to be? Are you expecting a terrific tomorrow, or are you dreading it? Your answer will have a powerful impact on the way tomorrow turns out.

Do you trust in the ultimate goodness of God's plan for your life? Will you face tomorrow's challenges with optimism and hope? You should. After all, God created you in His image for a very important reason: His reason. You have important work to do: His work.

As you live in the present and look to the future, remember that God has an amazing plan for you. All you have to do is believe and act accordingly, and He will guide you toward a brighter future than you can ever imagine.

"I know the plans I have for you"—
this is the LORD's declaration—
"plans for your well-being, not for disaster,
to give you a future and a hope."

JEREMIAH 29:11 CSB

FOCUS ON BEING DISCIPLINED

Wise women understand the importance of discipline. In Proverbs 28:19, the message is clear: "Those who work their land will have plenty of food, but the other ones who chase empty dreams instead will end up poor" (NCV). If we work diligently and faithfully, we can expect a bountiful harvest. But we must never expect the harvest to precede the labor.

Thoughtful women understand there is no reward for laziness or misbehavior. God gently guides His children (of all ages) to lead disciplined lives that strengthen hearts, minds, and souls while serving as positive examples to all. When we develop and apply discipline in our daily lives, God rewards us.

God doesn't want your life to be chaotic or exhausting. He will give you the discernment to recognize what is best for you, and He will help you develop the discipline necessary for a fulfilling life.

I discipline my body and bring it into subjection,
lest, when I have preached to others,
I myself should become disqualified.

1 CORINTHIANS 9:27

ASKING GOD TO
MEET YOUR NEEDS

God gives the gifts—we, as believers, simply receive them. But we don't always choose to. Why? Because we fail to trust our heavenly Father completely, and because we are sometimes more stubborn than we think. Luke 11 teaches us that God does not withhold spiritual gifts from those who ask. Our obligation, quite simply, is to ask for them.

Do you ask God to move mountains in your life while you stumble over molehills? Whatever the size of your challenges, God is big enough to handle them. Ask God to meet you where you are and meet your needs. Ask with faith and with fervor, and then watch in amazement as your mountains begin to move.

When we realize we're not troubling God when we bring Him our requests and concerns, we discover His heart is open to hear us—His touch nearer than our next thought—as if no one in the world existed but us. Our very personal God wants to hear from us personally.

You do not have because you do not ask.

James 4:2 csb

TRUSTING IN
GOD'S PROMISES

When our dreams come true and our plans prove successful, we find it easy to thank God and trust His divine providence. But in times of sorrow or hardship, we may find ourselves questioning God's plan for our lives.

Sometimes, we confront circumstances that trouble us to the core of our souls. During these difficult days, we must find the wisdom and the courage to trust our heavenly Father despite our circumstances.

Are you seeking God's blessings for you and your family? Then trust Him. Trust Him with your relationships. Trust Him with your priorities. Follow His commandments and pray for His guidance. Trust Him day by day, moment by moment—in good and bad times. Then, wait patiently for God's revelation... and prepare yourself for the abundance and peace that will most certainly be yours when you do.

*Trust in the LORD with all your heart, and do not rely on
your own understanding; in all your ways know him,
and he will make your paths straight.*

PROVERBS 3:5-6 CSB

GETTING BEYOND FEAR

A terrible storm rose quickly on the Sea of Galilee, and the disciples were afraid. Although they had witnessed many miracles, they feared for their lives, so they turned to Jesus and He calmed the waters and the wind.

Sometimes we, like Jesus's disciples, feel threatened by the storms of life. When we are fearful, we too should turn to Him for comfort and courage. The next time you feel yourself facing a fear-provoking situation, remember that the One who calmed the wind and the waves is also your personal Savior. He can calm any turbulent situation you are facing.

Ask yourself which is stronger—your faith or your fear? The answer should be obvious. So when the storm clouds form overhead and you find yourself being tossed on the strong seas of life, remember this: Wherever you are, God is there too. He cares for you and protects you.

If you fear God, then you have no reason to fear anything else. On the other hand, if a person does not fear God, then fear becomes a way of life.

Even when I go through the darkest valley,
I fear no danger, for you are with me.

PSALM 23:4 CSB

RELYING ON
PATIENCE AND TRUST

Psalm 37:7 commands us to wait patiently for God. But as busy women in a fast-paced world, many of us find that waiting quietly for God is difficult. Why? Because we are fallible human beings seeking to live according to our own schedules, not God's timetable. In our better moments, we realize that patience is not only a virtue but also a commandment from God.

We are impatient by nature. We know what we want, and we know when we want it: Now! But God knows better. He has created a world that unfolds according to His plans, not our own. As believers, we must trust His wisdom and His goodness.

God instructs us to be patient in all things. We must be patient with our families, our friends, and our associates. We must also be patient with God as He unfolds His plan for our lives. After all, think how patient God has been with us.

Trust in Him at all times, you people;
pour out your heart before Him;
God is a refuge for us.

PSALM 62:8

ARE YOU STILL GROWING?

When will you be a fully grown Christian woman? Can you ever be 100 percent mature in your faith? Even though it would be incredible to achieve, our spiritual growth doesn't end until we arrive in heaven. Living here on earth, we're never fully grown. We always have the potential to keep growing.

In those quiet moments when you open your heart to God, the One who made you keeps remaking you. He gives you direction, perspective, wisdom, and courage.

Would you like a time-tested formula for spiritual growth? Here it is: Keep studying God's Word, keep obeying His commandments, keep praying (and listening for answers), and keep trying to live in the center of God's will. When you do, you'll never stay stuck for long. Instead, you will continue to grow in Christ, and that's precisely the kind of Christian God wants you to be.

When it comes to your faith, God doesn't intend for you to stand still. He wants you to keep moving forward and growing.

Let us leave the elementary teaching
about Christ and go on to maturity.

Hebrews 6:1 csb

A COMMITMENT
TO FOLLOW HIM

Jesus walks with you. Are you walking with Him? Hopefully, you will choose to walk with Him today and every day.

Jesus loves you so much, He endured unspeakable humiliation and suffering on the cross. How will you respond to Christ's sacrifice? Will you take up His cross and follow Him (Luke 9:23), or will you choose another path? When you place your hopes squarely at the foot of the cross and place Jesus squarely at the center of your life, you will be blessed. If you seek to be a worthy disciple of Jesus, you must acknowledge that He never comes "next." He is always first.

Do you hope to fulfill God's purpose for your life? Do you seek a life of abundance and peace? Do you intend to be a Christian, not just in name, but in deed? Then follow Christ. Follow Him by picking up His cross daily in the way you live your life. When you do, you will quickly discover that Christ's love has the power to change everything, including you.

If anyone serves Me, let him follow Me;
and where I am, there My servant will be also.
If anyone serves Me, him My Father will honor.

JOHN 12:26

MAKING CHOICES

Life is a series of choices. Each day, we make countless decisions that can bring us closer to God...or not. When we live according to God's commandments, we make ourselves available to receive the abundance and peace He longs to give us. But when we disobey Him, we bring needless suffering upon ourselves and others.

Do you seek spiritual abundance that can be yours through Jesus Christ? Then invite Him into your heart and live according to His teachings. And when you confront a difficult decision or a powerful temptation, seek God's insights and follow them. When you do, you will receive untold blessings—now and for all eternity.

I have set before you life and death, blessing and curse.
Choose life so that you and your descendants may live,
love the LORD your God, obey him, and remain faithful
to him. For he is your life, and he will prolong your
days as you live in the land the LORD swore to give
to your ancestors Abraham, Isaac, and Jacob.

DEUTERONOMY 30:19-20 CSB

FINDING CONTENTMENT

Where can you find contentment? Is it a result of wealth, or power, or beauty, or fame? Hardly. Genuine contentment comes from a peaceful spirit, a clear conscience, and a loving heart.

Our world seems preoccupied with the search for happiness. We are bombarded with messages telling us happiness depends on acquiring material possessions. These messages are false. Enduring peace is not the result of our acquisitions; it is the inevitable result of our dispositions. If we don't find contentment within ourselves, we will never find it outside ourselves.

The search for contentment is an internal quest, an exploration of the heart, mind, and soul. You can find contentment if you simply look in the right places, and the best time to start looking in those places is now.

God offers you His peace, His protection, and His promises. If you accept these gifts, you will be content and find fulfillment.

I am the door. If anyone enters by Me, he will be saved,
and will go in and out and find pasture.

JOHN 10:9

PURPOSEFUL LIVING

What on earth does God intend for me to do with my life? For many of us, the question is easy to ask but difficult to answer. Why? Because God's purposes aren't always clear to us. Sometimes we wander aimlessly in a wilderness of our own making. And sometimes, we struggle mightily against God in an unsuccessful attempt to find success and happiness through our own means, not His.

If you sincerely seek God's guidance, He will give it. But He will make His revelations known to you in a way and in a time of His choosing, not yours. So be patient and wait on God's timing. If you prayerfully petition God and work diligently to discern His intentions, He will, in time, lead you to a place of joyful abundance and eternal peace.

Sometimes God's intentions will be clear to you. Other times, His plan will seem fuzzy. But even on those difficult days when you are unsure which way to turn, remember that God created you for a reason, He has important work for you to do, and He's waiting patiently for you to do it. The next step is up to you.

Whatever you do, do all to the glory of God.

1 Corinthians 10:31

FLEE FROM TEMPTATION

It's a hard truth: We live in a temptation-filled world. Every day, the devil is hard at work causing us pain and heartache. The enemy is working around the clock to lead us astray. That's why we must remain strong and vigilant.

In a letter to believers, Peter offered a stern warning: "Your adversary, the devil, prowls around like a roaring lion, seeking someone to devour" (1 Peter 5:8 NASB). What was true in New Testament times is equally true today. Satan tempts his prey and then devours them. As believing Christians, we must beware. We should live righteously and wrap ourselves in the protection of God's holy Word. When we do, we are secure.

Because we live in a temptation-filled world, let's guard our eyes, our thoughts, and our hearts—all day, every day.

The Lord knows how to deliver the godly out of temptations.

2 PETER 2:9

ALLOW GOD TO LEAD

The Bible promises that God will guide you if you let Him. Your job, of course, is to let Him. But sometimes, you will be tempted to do otherwise. Sometimes, you'll be tempted to go along with the crowd. Other times, you'll be tempted to do things your way, not God's way. When you feel those temptations, resist them.

What will you allow to guide you through the coming day—your own desires? Or will you allow God to lead the way?

When you entrust your life to Him completely, God will give you the strength to meet any challenge, the courage to face any trial, and the wisdom to live in His righteousness. So trust Him today and seek His guidance. When you do, your next step will be the right one.

Allow God to guide you today and every day. When you pray for guidance, God will give it.

The true children of God are those
who let God's Spirit lead them.

Romans 8:14 ncv

PRAYERS FOR
GOD'S ABUNDANCE

The familiar words of John 10:10 serve as a daily reminder: Christ came to the earth so we might experience His abundance, His love, and His gift of eternal life. However, Christ does not force Himself upon us—we must claim His gifts for ourselves.

Every woman knows that some days are so busy and so hurried that abundance seems a distant promise. It is not. Every day we can claim the spiritual abundance God promises for our lives—and we should.

Hannah Whitall Smith spoke for believers of every generation when she observed, "God is the giver and we are the receivers. And His richest gifts are bestowed not upon those who do the greatest things, but upon those who accept His abundance and His grace." Christ is indeed the Giver.

Will you accept His gifts? God wants to shower you with abundance—your job is to let Him.

I have come that they may have life,
and that they may have it more abundantly.

John 10:10

TRUSTING IN
GOD'S WISDOM

Where do you place your trust? Do you trust in the wisdom of fallible men and women, or do you place your faith in God's perfect wisdom? Knowing whom to trust is one of the best ways to successfully navigate life's challenges.

Do you find yourself feeling weary, discouraged, even fearful? Be comforted and trust God. Are you worried or anxious? Be confident in God's power and trust His holy Word. Are you confused? Listen to the quiet voice of your heavenly Father. He is not a God of confusion. Talk with Him, listen to Him, and trust Him. He is steadfast, and He is your Protector, today and forever.

God's wisdom is perfect, and it's available to you. So if you want to become wise, become a student of God's Word and follow the example of His Son.

Insight is a fountain of life for its possessor,
but the discipline of fools is folly.

PROVERBS 16:22 CSB

OUR APPEARANCE TO GOD

Are you worried about keeping up appearances? Do you spend too much time, energy, or money on things that make you look good? If so, you are certainly not alone. We live in a society that focuses on appearances. We are told over and over that we can't be "too thin or too wealthy." But in truth, the important things in life have little to do with fashion, fame, or fortune.

Here's a quick challenge: Today, spend less time trying to please the world and more time trying to please your earthly family and your heavenly Father. Focus on pleasing your God and your loved ones, and don't worry too much about trying to impress the people you interact with or pass on the street. It takes too much energy—and too much life—to keep up appearances. So don't waste your energy or your life.

How you appear to other people doesn't make much difference, but how you appear to God makes all the difference.

Humans do not see what the LORD sees,
for humans see what is visible,
but the LORD sees the heart.

1 SAMUEL 16:7 CSB

CELEBRATING LIFE

Psalm 100:1 reminds us the entire earth should "shout for joy to the Lord" (NIV). As God's children, we are blessed beyond measure, but sometimes, as busy women living in a demanding world, we are slow to count our gifts and even slower to thank God for them.

Our blessings include life and health, family and friends, freedom and possessions, and much more. The gifts we receive from God are multiplied when we share them. May we always give thanks to God for His blessings, and may we always demonstrate our gratitude by sharing our gifts with others.

Another Psalm reminds us, "This the day which the Lord has made; let's rejoice and be glad in it" (Psalm 118:24 NASB). Let's celebrate this day and the One who created it for us. In fact, every day is worth celebrating. By celebrating the gift of life, you protect your heart from the dangers of regret, hopelessness, and bitterness.

> *I know also, my God, that You test the heart and have*
> *pleasure in uprightness. As for me, in the uprightness*
> *of my heart I have willingly offered all these things;*
> *and now with joy I have seen Your people, who*
> *are present here to offer willingly to You.*
>
> 1 Chronicles 29:17

THERE'S POWER IN FAITH

When a suffering woman sought healing by simply touching the hem of His garment, Jesus turned and said, "Daughter, cheer up! Your faith has made you well" (Matthew 9:22 NLT). We too can be made whole when we place our faith completely in Jesus Christ.

Concentration camp survivor Corrie ten Boom relied on faith during her ten months of imprisonment and torture. Sadly, four of her family members died in Nazi death camps, yet Corrie's faith was unshaken. She wrote, "There is no pit so deep that God's love is not deeper still." Let's remember that genuine faith in God means faith in all circumstances, happy or sad, joyful or tragic.

If your faith is being tested to the breaking point, take heart. Your Savior is near. If you reach out to Him in faith, He will give you peace and heal your broken spirit. Be content to touch even the smallest fragment of the Master's garment, and He will make you whole.

Whatever is born of God overcomes the world. And this is the victory that has overcome the world—our faith.

1 John 5:4

ACCEPTANCE IS A CHOICE

Sometimes we must accept life on its terms, not on ours. Life has a way of unfolding as it will rather than as we would like it to. And sometimes, there is little we can do to change the circumstances facing us.

When life seems out of control, we have a choice: We can learn the art of acceptance, or we can make ourselves miserable as we struggle to change the unchangeable. Let's learn to entrust to God the things we cannot change. This frees us to prayerfully and faithfully do the important work He has chosen for us: doing something about the things we can change.

When we encounter situations we cannot change, let's look at them as opportunities to trust God more. Today, ask God for the courage and the wisdom to accept life on its own terms.

A person's heart plans his way,
but the LORD determines his steps.

PROVERBS 16:9 CSB

YOUR WISH LIST

What's on your wish list right now? For many, money and material possessions top the list. Americans have a possession obsession: We want faster computers, cooler cars, and smarter smartphones.

Seeking "the good life" isn't inherently bad—as long as this quest is secondary to "the truly meaningful life." Unfortunately, the drive for material possessions can become all-consuming—a shallow, self-gratifying obsession with no lasting significance.

Today's truly content women have learned to travel light. They see life as a journey and resolve to take with them *only* the bare essentials. They don't want the burden of unnecessary baggage. They don't get distracted by the glitter of money or the aura of fame and power.

They ignore the extraneous shiny stuff because they have God's inner light—a light so brilliant, it makes everything else dull in comparison. This light, one of love and purpose, is the light that will help us find and navigate the path of true happiness and fulfillment. Let's allow God's light to guide us always.

> *You're blessed when you're content with*
> *just who you are—no more, no less. That's the*
> *moment you find yourselves proud owners*
> *of everything that can't be bought.*
>
> MATTHEW 5:5 MSG

THE JOY IN FELLOWSHIP

Fellowship with other believers is one of life's greatest blessings. Our fellow Christians uplift us, encourage us, and enlighten us. Being a consistent and active member of a fellowship builds bridges inside the four walls of your church and provides opportunities for outreach and connection beyond them.

Do you serve God by sharing your time and your talents with a close-knit band of believers? Do you seek ways to spread God's good news to your community and beyond?

Fellowship with others is part of God's plan for our lives. We need that camaraderie with other people of faith. And your Christian friends need fellowship with *you*.

*He keeps us in step with each other. His very breath
and blood flow through us, nourishing us so that
we will grow up healthy in God, robust in love.*

Ephesians 4:16 msg

GOD'S PERFECT TIMING

Trusting in God's timing can make a huge difference in our faith journeys. As fallible beings, we can become impatient. But we should remember that God knows better than we do, and He always has our back.

God created a world that unfolds according to His own timetable, not ours. Thank goodness, right? We sometimes make bad choices, but God never does.

As believers, our task is to believe in the all-knowing Father and be patient for Him to reveal Himself—because He will. As God's perfect plan unfolds, let's walk in faith and never lose hope. Let's continue to trust Him always.

After all, we don't always know what we need or when we need it, but God does. Rest assured, you can trust Him and His timing for you.

Humble yourselves under the mighty hand of God,
that He may exalt you in due time.

1 Peter 5:6

CHOOSE TO BE KIND

Christ showed His love for us by willingly sacrificing His life so we may have eternal life: "But God demonstrates his own love for us in this: While we were still sinners, Christ died for us" (Romans 5:8 NIV). As Christian followers, we are challenged to share His love with kind words on our lips and praise in our hearts.

Christ has been and always will be the ultimate Shepherd to His flock. We can follow Him by showing kindness and generosity to others, especially those who are most in need.

When we walk each day with Jesus and obey His commandments, we become effective ambassadors for Christ. When we spread the love of Christ, we share a priceless gift with the world. That's what servants of God do! Kind words and actions have echoes that last a lifetime and beyond.

May the Lord make you increase and
abound in love to one another and to all.

1 THESSALONIANS 3:12

BE CHEERFUL

Life's twists and turns can make it hard to be cheerful. As the demands of the world increase, we can feel as if our energy is depleted, and we are less likely to "cheer up" and more likely to "tear up." But even in our darkest hours, we can turn to God, and He will give us comfort.

Few things in life are sadder (or more absurd) than a grumpy Christian. Christ promises us lives of abundance and joy, but He does not force His joy upon us. He allows us to choose and claim joy for ourselves. When we do, Jesus fills our spirits with His power and His love.

We receive from Christ the joy that is rightfully ours as we give Him what is rightfully His: our hearts and our souls. Remember, God is good and heaven is forever. If those two facts don't cheer you up, nothing will.

What a relief to see your friendly smile.
It is like seeing the face of God!

Genesis 33:10 NLT

GROWING
CLOSER TO JESUS

Whom do you trust most?

Did a best friend's name spring to mind? Or did you think of Jesus? When you form a life-changing relationship with Him, He'll be your best friend forever. He won't leave your side, and you can count on Him when you can't rely on anyone else.

Jesus wants to share the gifts of everlasting life and love with you. When you make a mistake, He'll stand by you. If you fall short of His commandments, He'll still love you. If you feel lonely or worried, He can touch your heart and lift your spirits.

Jesus wants you to enjoy a happy, healthy, and abundant life. He wants you to walk with Him and share His good news. Jesus is the light of the world, and that includes your world. Be open to His love for you, and your love for Him and your relationship with Him will naturally grow.

In the beginning was the Word, and the Word was with God,
and the Word was God…And the Word was made flesh,
and dwelt among us, (and we beheld his glory, the glory as
of the only begotten of the Father,) full of grace and truth.

JOHN 1:1,14 KJV

TAKE CONTROL OF
YOUR THOUGHTS

Thoughts are powerful. Our thoughts have the power to lift us up or drag us down. They have the power to energize us or deplete us, to inspire us to greater accomplishments or to make those accomplishments seem impossible.

Bishop Fulton Sheen observed, "The mind is like a clock that is constantly running down. It needs to be wound up daily with good thoughts." But sometimes, even for the most faithful believers, winding up our intellectual clocks is difficult.

If negative thoughts have left you worried, exhausted, or both, it's time to readjust your thought patterns. Negative thinking is habit forming. Thankfully, so is positive thinking. Let your mind be drawn to God's power and your possibilities. Both are far greater than you can imagine.

You can control your thoughts—they don't have to control you.

Finally brothers and sisters, whatever is true, whatever
is honorable, whatever is just, whatever is pure,
whatever is lovely, whatever is commendable—
if there is any moral excellence and if there is
anything praiseworthy—dwell on these things.

PHILIPPIANS 4:8 CSB

DON'T LET
YOURSELF WORRY

If you are like most women, worry is part of your life. You worry about health, about finances, about safety, about relationships, about family, and about countless other challenges of life—some great, some small. Where is the best place to take your worries? Take them to God. Take your troubles to Him—and your fears and your sorrows. He will accept them all.

Worry clutters up tomorrow's opportunities with today's leftover problems. So if you'd like to make the most out of this day (and every day), give your worries to the One who is greater than you are and spend your valuable time and energy solving the problems you can fix.

When you find yourself consumed with worry, try this simple formula: Work hard, pray harder, and leave your worries with God for Him to handle.

Don't worry about anything, but in everything,
through prayer and petition with thanksgiving,
present your requests to God.

PHILIPPIANS 4:6 CSB

SEEKING AND STUDYING
SCRIPTURAL TRUTHS

As a spiritual being, you can know the Lord better every day. You can do so through prayer, through worship, through an openness to God's Holy Spirit, and through careful study of His holy Word.

Your Bible contains powerful prescriptions for everyday living. If you sincerely seek to walk with God, it's wise to commit yourself to the thoughtful study of His teachings. The Bible should be your road map for every aspect of your life.

Do you want a closer relationship with your heavenly Father? Then study His Word daily with a spirit of eagerness to be inspired and to learn. The Bible is a priceless, one-of-a-kind gift from God. Read and discover its many treasures.

Remember, you're never too young or too old to become a serious student of God's Word and apply it to your daily life.

Faith comes by hearing, and hearing by the word of God.

Romans 10:17

ENVY

In a competitive, cutthroat world, it is easy to envy others' successes. But it's wrong. We know intuitively that envy is wrong, but because we are frail, imperfect human beings, we may find ourselves struggling with feelings of envy or resentment or both. These feelings may be especially strong when we see other people experience unusually good fortune.

Have you recently felt the pangs of envy creeping into your heart? If so, it's time to focus on the marvelous things God has done for you and your family. And just as importantly, try not to preoccupy yourself with the blessings God has chosen to give others.

So, for a happier and healthier life, remember to count your blessings—and to let your neighbors count theirs.

Let us walk properly, as in the day, not in revelry and drunkenness, not in lewdness and lust, not in strife and envy.

ROMANS 13:13

EMBRACING GOD'S LOVE

Life was not easy for the psalmist David. King Saul was determined to kill him, and David was forced to hide in a cave. But even in that dark place, the light of God's love shined in his heart: "I will praise you, Lord, among the nations; I will sing of you among the peoples. For great is your love, reaching to the heavens; your faithfulness reaches to the skies" (Psalm 57:9-10 NIV).

God made you in His image and gave you salvation through His Son, Jesus Christ. As a wondrous creation treasured by God, how will you respond to the Creator's love? Will you ignore it or embrace it? Will you return it or neglect it? God has left that decision up to you.

When you embrace God's love, your life is forever changed. You feel different about yourself, your neighbors, your family, and the world around you. Most importantly, you share God's message and His love with others. Your heavenly Father—a God of infinite love and mercy—is waiting to embrace you with open arms. Remember to accept His love each and every day.

> *This is My commandment, that you*
> *love one another as I have loved you.*
>
> JOHN 15:12

ENCOURAGE OTHERS

Do you strive to be a continuing source of encouragement to your family and friends? Hopefully so. After all, one of the reasons God put you here is to serve and encourage others—starting with those closest to you.

In his letter to the Ephesians, Paul wrote, "Do not let any unwholesome talk come out of your mouths, but only what is helpful for building others up according to their needs, that it may benefit those who listen" (Ephesians 4:29 NIV). This passage reminds us that we should choose our words carefully as we build others up through wholesome, honest encouragement.

How can we build others up? By celebrating their victories and their accomplishments. As the old saying goes, "When someone does something good, applaud—you'll make two people happy." Today, look for the good in others and celebrate the good you find. When you do, you'll be a powerful force of encouragement in your corner of the world, as well as a worthy servant to your God.

Patience and encouragement come from God.
And I pray that God will help you all agree
with each other the way Christ Jesus wants.

ROMANS 15:5 ICB

THE WISDOM IN
BEING GENEROUS

The thread of generosity is woven into the fabric of Christ's teachings. As He sent His disciples to heal the sick and spread God's message of salvation, Jesus offered this guiding principle: "Freely you have received, freely give" (Matthew 10:8). The principle still applies. As disciples of Christ, we should give freely of our time, our possessions, and our love.

When the Lord blesses us abundantly, we don't always remember to thank Him. And sometimes we neglect to "pay it forward" and bless others as God has blessed us.

All of us have been blessed at various times in our lives, and we are called to share those blessings without reservation. The world needs our help, and when we freely share our possessions, our talents, and our time, the wonderful cycle of blessing continues.

Freely you have received, freely give.

MATTHEW 10:8

GOD-DIRECTED HAPPINESS

How do we know we are living right with God? First, of course, we accept His Son into our lives. Then we begin guiding our lives by God's commandments. Accepting Christ is a one-time decision for most of us, but following in Jesus's footsteps brings us the challenge of making dozens of conscious decisions, large and small, every day.

Each morning presents questions: "Whose steps will I follow today? Will I honor God by living by Jesus's example? Or will I follow the crowd that chases happiness and fulfillment down a road that leads only to pain and disappointment?"

God is holy, and He wants us to be holy. He also loves us, and obeying Him is one way of saying, "I love You too, heavenly Father."

God *is* love. He wants love to be the root and foundation of our lives. Living in love and holiness is not about keeping track of how many rules we've followed or how "godly" we feel. Instead, God wants us to live lives that emanate peace, joy, and love—for our family, friends, and neighbors. He wants us to enjoy the blessings that come from *deciding* to live in the security and hope of our Savior.

Since everything here today might well be gone tomorrow,
do you see how essential it is to live a holy life?

2 Peter 3:11 msg

PRIORITIES IN PLACE

Books and blogs abound on subjects like setting priorities, time management, and strategic planning. But how many of us ask God to help prioritize our lives? Do we seek Him for guidance and for the courage to do the things that need to be done? Consider this: As we align our priorities with God's, we invite our Creator to reveal Himself in a variety of ways. We open ourselves to a world of holy possibilities.

By making God's priorities *our* priorities, we receive His abundance and His peace. With God as our full partner in life, we have the assurance that we are following His path, which is always the best path. When God rules in our hearts, He showers us with spiritual blessings—too many to count.

As we plan for the day ahead, let's make God's will our ultimate priority. Once God has the top spot, the other priorities are easier to move to their proper places. Our priorities matter, because the priorities we set determine the course of our lives. So why not set priorities carefully and carry them out intentionally and consistently—God's way?

If anyone desires to come after Me, let him deny
himself, and take up his cross daily, and follow Me.
For whoever desires to save his life will lose it, but
whoever loses his life for My sake will save it.

LUKE 9:23-24

COUNT YOUR
(MANY) BLESSINGS

Psalm 145 promises us, "The LORD is gracious and compassionate, slow to anger and rich in love. The LORD is good to all; he has compassion on all he has made" (verses 8-9 NIV). As God's children, we are blessed beyond measure, but sometimes we are slow to count our gifts and to thank the Giver.

Our blessings include life and love, family and friends, freedom and hope. And the gifts we receive from God are multiplied when we share them with others. May we always thank God for our blessings and may demonstrate our gratitude by sharing them.

Jesus wants us to experience abundant blessings every day. He said, "I have come that they may have life, and that they may have it more abundantly" (John 10:10).

Even though we all face challenges, we are truly blessed by God. What a comfort that is. May we always be thankful for blessings large and small.

I will make you a great nation; I will bless you and make
your name great; and you shall be a blessing. I will bless
those who bless you, and I will curse him who curses you;
and in you all the families of the earth shall be blessed.

GENESIS 12:2-3

BEING DISCIPLES
OF CHRIST

Jesus challenged His disciples to "take up their cross" and follow Him (Matthew 16:24 NIV). They must have understood the weight of those words. In Jesus's day, condemned prisoners were forced to carry the crossbeams of their crosses to the place of execution. Jesus wanted His disciples to understand that they needed to deny their own desires and trust in Him completely—even in times of pain, fear, and despair. We face the same challenge, and the same opportunities, today.

As Jesus's disciples, we lovingly trust Him and place Him at the center of our beings. In other words, Jesus never comes "next." He is always our first. The wonderful irony is that when we give of ourselves to Him, He gives us the gift of salvation—the greatest gift of all.

Jesus gives us all we need to be His disciples. When we feel too discouraged or tired to walk another step, He provides the strength to carry on. Imagine that: Jesus invites us to the privilege of being disciples, and then He enables us to live out that privilege every day.

*Jesus said unto them, Come ye after me, and I will
make you to become fishers of men. And straightway
they forsook their nets, and followed him.*

MARK 1:17-18 KJV

GOD LOVES YOU!

Because God's power is limitless, our mortal minds cannot fully appreciate it. The same is true of God's love. We can't fully understand or appreciate the scope of God's love, but, thankfully, we can *experience* it.

God's love knows no bounds. It's not a limited resource. The love that flows to us from God's heart is infinite—like a wellspring that never runs dry. Today, we have yet another opportunity to celebrate that love and to share it.

As a woman, you are a glorious creation, a unique individual, a beautiful example of God's handiwork. God's love for you is limitless. Let's accept that love and be grateful for it. And remember, when all else fails, God's love never does. You can always depend on His love. He is your ultimate protector and caregiver.

Our loving God deals with us mercifully, and that makes all the difference. Let's praise God, whose great love ensures that "we are not consumed, for his compassions never fail" (Lamentations 3:22 NIV).

God so loved the world, that he gave his
only begotten Son, that whosoever believeth in him
should not perish, but have everlasting life.

JOHN 3:16 KJV

FOLLOWING
CHRIST'S EXAMPLE

Whether we like it or not, all of us are role models. Our friends and family members watch our actions and, as followers of Christ, we should remember this. Do you ever ask yourself, "What kind of example am I?" Does your life serve as a genuine example of righteousness? Are you a positive role model for young people? Do you speak and act with kindness, faithfulness, and love for the Lord?

If so, you are blessed by God, and you're a powerful force for good in a world that desperately needs positive influences such as yours. Corrie ten Boom advised, "Don't worry about what you do not understand. Worry about what you do understand in the Bible but do not live by." This is sound advice because our families and friends are watching, and so is God.

God wants us to be good role models. Let's make this goal our hearts' desire as well.

Be an example to the believers in word,
in conduct, in love, in spirit, in faith, in purity.

1 Timothy 4:12

TRUTH FOR ALL TIME

Pilate, the Roman governor of Judea, asked Jesus, "What is truth?" (John 18:38). His rhetorical question and cynical tone echo loudly through the ages. Had he been privileged to be with Jesus and the disciples the evening before in the upper room, he would have known the answer.

Jesus had told His friends, "I am the way, the truth, and the life" (John 14:6).

In other words, truth is a Person.

And because Jesus lives forever, God's revelation of truth in Him is eternal. The truth you trusted when you first put your faith in Christ is the truth that will lead and guide you throughout your life. The truth we teach our children when they are young is the same truth that will guide them when they are older.

As we spend the rest of our lives (and perhaps eternity!) learning more about the truth, we can be confident we are building the foundations of our lives on the solid rock—ultimate truth revealed in the words and works of Jesus Christ.

When He, the Spirit of truth, has come,
He will guide you into all truth.

JOHN 16:13

SMALL BLESSINGS
ARE A BIG DEAL

This morning, did your own private robot roll into your bedroom and wake you up by playing some of your favorite songs on his onboard, high-tech sound system?

Did a famous TV chef cook your breakfast?

The last time you took a trip, did you travel by private helicopter or stretch limousine?

The answer to these questions is probably no. But a life without a lot of fancy stuff can still be amazing. Every day, God provides dozens of small blessings we can enjoy if only we have the eyes to see them and the hearts to appreciate them.

The warmth of that special someone's smile. Watching a favorite TV show or movie with a couple of close friends. The beauty of a sunset. Hearing "Great work!" from a boss or coworker. The comfort of crawling into bed after a busy day.

Let's strive to remember that enjoying God's small blessings can make a so-called common life uncommonly good. The difference between an ordinary life and an extraordinary one is the "extra" care we take to appreciate all the ways God shows His love for us.

Make sure that your character is free from
the love of money, being content with what you have.

HEBREWS 13:5 NASB

GOD'S GREAT PURPOSE

God has a purpose for your life. His purpose for us has been in His heart since before the foundation of the world, and His concern for us was vibrant before we were ever conceived. Not one of His thoughts toward us or His promises to us has ever failed, nor will it.

When tough times come, and they will, it's hard to acknowledge that His purposes are good. But we should remember that God has always been there, taking us to places we never dreamed of and providing experiences we never thought we would enjoy.

How great is God's purpose for us! How wonderful it is to live out that purpose!

Not one thing has failed of all the good things
which the LORD your God spoke concerning you.
All have come to pass.

JOSHUA 23:14

GOD'S MASTER PLAN

God possesses some amazing powers: parting seas, magically providing food from heaven, and even raising the dead. But one of our Creator's more underrated powers is His ability to turn stumbling blocks into stepping-stones.

We've seen this truth play out in our lives and those of the people around us: One door of opportunity closes, but God opens another one. A failure mysteriously evolves into the key for later success. Bitter rejection becomes the fuel for a new level of focus and determination. As the Bible assures us, "In all things God works for the good of those who love him" (Romans 8:28 NIV).

Of course, those words from Paul's letter to the Romans does not mean that *everything* that happens to us is good. It does mean, however, that God can take the ugly things life hurls at us and somehow make them beautiful. He can bring us through the worst of times and make us stronger, more hopeful, and more grateful women in the process.

Whatever our life challenges might be, let's remember that God's plan for us just might include a Plan B…or even C.

I will never leave you nor forsake you.

HEBREWS 13:5

"WE INTERRUPT
THIS LIFE..."

It's amazing how minor irritations can take a woman's eyes off of God. Tension headaches interrupt our sleep. Telemarketing calls interrupt our dinnertime. Corporate restructurings interrupt our career progress, and workplace "emergencies" interrupt our vacations. To be fair, sometimes troubles on the home front interrupt us at work.

When we get a case of "life interrupted," it's smart to step back and regain our perspective. Will the world stop turning if we don't quite make that project deadline? Will babies no longer smile and birds no longer sing if we can't do absolutely everything we want while on vacation? Will our job become less meaningful if a less-deserving person gets associate of the month?

When we look at life clearly, what is a traffic ticket or flat tire or flight delay when we compare them to being loved wholly and eternally by Almighty God? What's more, what can possibly compare to being made clean from all of our sins? Even when life is hard, life is still good. Because our God is *good*.

Who of you by worrying can add
a single hour to your life?

MATTHEW 6:27 NIV

REAL LOVE

What is love? Scroll through your social media feed and the word pops up like dandelions.

Unfortunately, the love that permeates our culture often isn't the real deal. The love many people profess is selfish obsession, usually driven by physical attraction.

Yes, love is emotional. But it is also a decision, an act of the will. True love is caring about other people—your spouse, kids, parents, and (gulp) parents-in-law—even if your love isn't reciprocated or appreciated.

Real love is what Jesus displayed for the world when He chose to sacrifice Himself for us. And He made this choice knowing that no one deserved this great gift of love and that many would not accept it. Still, He gave His life.

The Lord of all creation, who knew you before you were born, has decided to love you. In spite of your mistakes. In spite of the indifference you might feel toward Him sometimes. God will faithfully forgive, unconditionally accept, and perfectly love you always.

Whoever does not love does not know God,
because God is love.

1 John 4:8 niv

HIGH WAYS

In our information-rich world, we have unraveled many of life's tangled mysteries. But there is much more that we *don't* understand. And just like a child who can't understand why she can't touch the moon or eat candy for every meal, we question God about things that don't make sense to us.

The Bible reminds us that God's ways are much higher than our ways and that we can comprehend only tiny slivers of His master plan. Our responsibility is to follow Him and trust that He can work out everything—even the bad things—for our good.

So let's learn to appreciate life's questions. And let's remember that God, the Master Architect of the universe, holds our hand. The road ahead might be unfamiliar and intimidating, but if you travel hand in hand with God, you'll find that the loving Father who walks beside you will get you where you need to go.

As the heavens are higher than the earth,
so are my ways higher than your ways
and my thoughts than your thoughts.

Isaiah 55:9 niv

GOD'S GIFTS

Magic moments. You've had them. Holding a little child's hand on a walk to the park or ice cream shop. Seeing that familiar smile burst across your best friend's face when you unexpectedly bump into each other at the coffee shop. Hearing a relative mention *your* name when thanking God for life's blessings.

Every moment like this is a gift. God has a way of sending these gifts to remind us there is more good in the world than bad. God offers a supply of love and kindness that will never run dry. And because of this, life is always worth living.

These gifts also remind us to keep our eyes, minds, and hearts open for the blessings, large and small, that await us in the future. So let's be watchful for those magic moments—the ones that fill our mouths with laughter and make us want to shout with joy.

So the next time life drops one of these blessings on your tongue, take time to savor it, enjoy it. A seemingly momentary blessing can leave a sweet aftertaste that can last forever—so let it.

Let the heavens rejoice, let the earth be glad;
let the sea resound, and all that is in it.

PSALM 96:11 NIV

EVERYDAY JOY

Has this ever happened to you? You've folded that last T-shirt, paid that last bill, or answered that last email. But then—instead of mentally checking another task off your to-do list or shaking your head at the monotony of daily life—you smile. You lean back and breathe deeply. You feel satisfied, centered.

True, you haven't cured any disease or solved world hunger, but you've done something well. You have made your home (your life) more organized and more efficient. *Better*. And for this, it's good to thank God.

Do you *love* every one of your daily tasks? Probably not. But can you do every task with love—love for a husband, a child, and life itself? Yes. Can you do it with love for the God who makes it all possible? Can you transform the mundane into the meaningful? Most definitely, yes.

When we are present in the everyday moments, we find that God is present with us.

For where your treasure is,
there your heart will be also.

Matthew 6:21

PROMISES, PROMISES

What is your immediate reaction when you hear a salesperson or politician say, "I promise"? An eye roll, perhaps, or a challenge to put that promise in writing. Because we have seen that mere words, no matter how sincerely they are uttered, can be hollow.

But when God declares allegiance to us, He shows us that He means it. The God who loves us is the same one who sets the stars in the night sky, follows winter with spring, and night with day. As Scripture says, "The heavens declare the glory of God; the skies proclaim the work of his hands" (Psalm 19:1 NIV).

When we open our eyes and our hearts, we see evidence of God's power, love, and faithfulness all around us. The comforting hug from a loved one. The melody of a favorite hymn. The pages of a book. And we are wise when we remember *how* God shows His love to us is not as important as the fact that He does indeed love us. He always will, because He is love. That's a promise we can always depend on.

I've banked your promises in the vault
of my heart.

PSALM 119:11 MSG

THE GOD GAP

A huge gap, a Grand Canyon, stands between knowing about God and truly *knowing* Him. Sometimes, God is like a movie. We've read the reviews, seen the previews. We can summarize the plot and quote a line or two of dialogue. We can even form a thumbs-up or thumbs-down opinion. But we haven't actually *experienced* the film.

Or perhaps God is like an exotic destination somewhere. We've visited the website, and the place sure looks inviting. But we've never been there.

God is our loving Creator, and He wants us to experience Him firsthand. Take time to simply be still in God's presence, and ask Him to fill your mind and your heart with His love.

As Richard Foster explains in his book *Life with God*, the main thread of the Bible is this promise and this invitation to real relationship with God: "I am with you. Will you be with Me?"

See how very much our Father loves us,
for he calls us his children.

1 John 3:1 nlt

WHO ARE YOU WHEN NOBODY'S WATCHING?

Your character is who you are when no one's watching. It's the best of you and the worst of you, all rolled into one. One of the goals of maturing as a woman is to get your character in line with who God created you to be.

Though there is no one quite like you, those who follow God share similar traits, such as honesty, integrity, generosity, and a deep-hearted love. These should be an essential part of who you are and how you live as God's child.

Character develops out of choice, not chance. Let's choose to work on erasing any traits that don't reflect God's character. Let's ask for God's help in developing the qualities most like His.

We show we are servants of God by our pure lives.

2 Corinthians 6:6 ncv

FINDING YOUR PLACE
IN THE FAMILY OF GOD

There's a community of believers out there that needs you. It isn't complete without you. What awaits is a support group of friends, opportunities to use the gifts God's given you, and an environment where you can grow. But you have to make the first move.

If your life has taken you in a new direction, don't put off finding a body of believers you can call home. If you're already part of a family of God, check your involvement level. If you're overinvolved or underinvolved, ask God to help you find a healthy balance. Then use your newfound freedom to make a wise choice to follow His leading. Honor God and feed your hungry soul by attending a weekly service. Go with a teachable mind and a servant's heart—and enjoy.

> *You should not stay away from the church meetings,*
> *as some are doing, but you should meet together*
> *and encourage each other.*
>
> HEBREWS 10:25 NCV

GOD IS NEAR

Everyone weeps. Even if your tears are not visible to those around you, life on this imperfect earth is bound to break your heart now and then. But you have a Father who loves you deeply. He doesn't want your heart to remain in shattered pieces. Like a mother who runs to her child's side the moment she hears a pain-filled cry, God is near, offering tender comfort when you need it most.

When your heart is crying out for healing, cry out to God. He'll never put you down for being overly emotional or tell you to grow up. Instead, He'll go to the source of your heartbreak, soothing your soul with peace and perspective. Allow God to dry your tears with His love.

The Lord wants to show his mercy to you.
He wants to rise and comfort you.
The Lord is a fair God, and everyone
who waits for his help will be happy.

Isaiah 30:18 ncv

FINDING YOUR LIFE'S WORK

A career is defined as a profession or vocation. It's more than just a job. Your career is your life's work. It should be something you love, something you feel you were born to do. Sounds simple—but it isn't always so easy to identify. If you feel that way, you aren't alone. Many people stop and start a few times before they find their truest calling.

No matter what, don't settle for less. Keep looking and trying new things until you find the best career path for you. You'll know it by the little leap your heart takes when you think and pray about it. You'll know because God will confirm it to you deep inside. Life is too short to spend it doing anything but what God has called you to do.

Each person has his own gift from God.
One has one gift, another has another gift.

1 Corinthians 7:7 ncv

SELF-ASSURANCE OR GOD-ASSURANCE?

A key rule of any job interview is to be confident of your strengths and experience. But where does that confidence come from? Is it found in your education? Your natural abilities? Your family connections? The new designer suit you happen to be wearing?

Confidence in anything other than God's love for you and His power working through you is not sturdy enough to build an accurate self-image on. Self-assurance is great, but God-assurance is what's going to keep you going through the ups and downs of life.

Our confidence in Christ awakens us, urges us on, and makes us active in living righteous lives and doing good. There is no self-confidence to compare with this.

When you're faced with a challenge, thank God for the strengths and assets He's provided you. Then, refuse to rely solely on them. Firmly place your confidence in God—in who He is and who He says you are in Him.

The LORD will be your confidence,
and will keep your foot from being caught.

PROVERBS 3:26

LETTING GO OF YOUR IDOLS

How much is enough? To a contented heart, it's as much as God has chosen to provide. To measure your personal level of contentment, complete this sentence: I would be content if only…

What are your "if onlys"? More money? Being involved in a serious relationship? Losing or gaining weight? Landing the job of your dreams?

There's another name for "if onlys." They're called idols. When your desires move from "it would be nice" to "I can't be happy without," you've chosen to believe some *thing* can satisfy you, instead of Someone. Ask God to reveal any "if onlys" you need to confront. Then, ask Him to show you how to find contentment where you are and with what you have right now.

The secret of contentment is the realization that life is a gift, not a right.

I have learned in whatever state I am, to be content.

Philippians 4:11

SEEKING GOD'S ADVICE

When you're faced with a tough decision, it's natural to go to a friend for advice. Chatting openly with someone who knows you and your situation can help you put the pros and cons of your options into clearer perspective. So what could make more sense than spending time talking things over with the One who knows you better than anyone else?

God cares about the direction of your life. The decisions you make each day help determine that direction. Weighing your decisions by what's written in the Bible and using the wisdom that God provides for the asking will not only help you determine right from wrong, but better from best.

You guide me with your advice,
and later you will receive me in honor.

Psalm 73:24 ncv

STANDING UP
TO LIFE'S GIANTS

It takes courage to go where God leads. He'll often take you right to the doorstep of your greatest fears, put you face to face with someone you can't stand to be around, or bring a challenging situation into your life. Don't panic. Those are the times when you can really see God's power in action.

You were never created to handle tough times alone. Consider David. The only reason he could conquer a giant was that God was with him. You have the same advantage. God is fighting every battle with you, never against you.

Joshua 1:9 reminds us, "Be strong and of good courage; do not be afraid, nor be dismayed, for the LORD your God is with you wherever you go." So take courage. Stand up to the giants in your life. With God's help, victory is at hand.

> *Don't lose your courage or be afraid. Don't panic or*
> *be frightened, because the LORD your God goes with you,*
> *to fight for you against your enemies and to save you.*
>
> DEUTERONOMY 20:3-4 NCV

DON'T GIVE UP

Have you ever wondered if life is worth the trouble? After all, it seems to be filled with heartache and disappointment and frustration. Sometimes, it's just plain boring and exhausting. God understands that you will sometimes feel like giving up. But He wants you to keep on going, refusing to quit until you have fulfilled the purpose for which He created you. That is determination.

God knows that every day of your life is important and worth living. One day there will be sweet rest. But for now, God is urging you to set your course and determine to see it through. And you should know that He is even more determined than you could ever be to see you finish the race He's set for you.

When you make a total effort, even when the odds are against you, never quit trying. Victory might be just around the corner.

Do not cast away your confidence, which has great reward.
For you have need of endurance, so that after you have
done the will of God, you may receive the promise.

HEBREWS 10:35-36

BEING AN ENCOURAGER

Encouragement is more than building others up with your words. It's helping them find the courage to move ahead in a positive direction.

When God opens your eyes to someone who's discouraged, disappointed, or in need of comfort, ask Him for the wisdom to know the best words and actions to share. Then, let God's love for you encourage your own heart so you can reach out in confidence, kindness, and humility.

Whatever you do or say, remember that it's God's love and power working through you that ultimately help another person—not your own superior counseling abilities. When God uses you in the lives of others, always thank Him for the privilege of being an encourager.

Allow encouragement to inspire and fuel your soul like oxygen in your lungs.

May our Lord Jesus Christ himself and
God our Father encourage you and strengthen you
in every good thing you do and say.

2 Thessalonians 2:16-17 ncv

STANDING IN BELIEF

Belief is not the absence of doubt, but the decision to stand in the midst of your doubts. Thomas had his doubts when the other disciples told him that Jesus had risen from the dead. But when Jesus appeared, He didn't condemn Thomas. Instead, He gave him evidence. He encouraged Thomas to touch Him and believe.

God doesn't condemn you for your doubts either. He just wants you to reach out to Him—to let Him prove to you that He does indeed exist. He desires to win you with His love and draw you with His kindness. Bring your doubts to Jesus; lay them at His feet in prayer. Let Him turn your doubts to belief.

God has never turned away someone who searches for belief. Healthy questions keep our faith dynamic. Doubts can prompt us to explore and find truth that leads us to a deep-rooted faith.

[Jesus] said to Thomas, "Reach your finger here, and look at
My hands; and reach your hand here, and put it into
My side. Do not be unbelieving, but believing."

JOHN 20:27

GOD'S POWER
WORKS WONDERS

God is all-powerful. When we hear about God's power we often think about wonders and miracles. These get people's attention. His miraculous power can draw large crowds, cause people to travel long distances, and stir up great excitement. The Bible gives us many glimpses into God's wonder-working power—healing a sick body (Mark 1:30-31), turning water into wine (John 2:9), feeding a multitude (Matthew 14:19), calming a stormy sea (Matthew 8:27), and raising the dead (John 11:43).

Wonders and miracles are manifestations of God's power that glorify Him, but they are not the only way God's power is revealed to us. In Ephesians 3:20, Paul described the power of God that works *within us*. Here, the emphasis is not upon what God's power can do *for* us, but what God's power can do *to* us. Sadly, the subject of miracles typically draws more attention than the subject of sanctification. There are many who will seek God for a new manifestation but will not seek Him for a new disposition; for a new sign, but not for a new heart; for a new wonder, but not for a new life. How will you seek God today?

To Him who is able to do exceedingly abundantly above all that
we ask or think, according to the power that works in us…

EPHESIANS 3:20

GOD'S POWER
CHANGES US

It takes the power of God to make a crippled man walk, to open the eyes of someone who cannot see, to bring hearing to deaf ears, and to set someone free from demonic powers. But it also takes the power of God to stop someone from grumbling and complaining, from being impatient, from giving up, from being ungrateful, or from being controlled by wrong attitudes.

We experience God's power to change us when we are cleansed by the blood of Jesus Christ, when we take up our cross and embrace His will, when we are filled and controlled by the Holy Spirit, when we walk in obedience to His Word, and when we trust Him with all our hearts.

> *[We pray] that you may walk worthy of the Lord, fully pleasing Him, being fruitful in every good work and increasing in the knowledge of God; strengthened with all might, according to His glorious power, for all patience and long-suffering with joy; giving thanks to the Father who has qualified us to be partakers of the inheritance of the saints in the light.*
>
> Colossians 1:10-12

GOD'S POWER IS AVAILABLE TO US

People can be *touched* by the power of God without being *changed* by it. (The account of the healing of the ten lepers in Luke 17:12-19 illustrates this.) As wonderful as it is to experience God's supernatural power through wonders and miracles, we must also trust in God's transforming power to live meaningful, victorious lives.

It takes God's power to remain on a task when you know it is not time to move on, to get the job done when you don't feel like it, to be faithful when other things want to pull you away, to do what's right when no one is watching, to be full of joy when you would rather mope, to keep gratitude in your heart when you would rather complain, to continue in hope when things around you are dark.

Each of us needs God's power to live a godly life, and thankfully, that power is available to us.

His divine power has given to us all things that pertain
to life and godliness, through the knowledge of Him
who called us by glory and virtue.

2 PETER 1:3

THERE'S SOMETHING DIFFERENT ABOUT YOU

In uncertain times, you are secure. While others walk in fear, you walk by faith. In a world that is like sand, your feet stand upon a rock. With worry all around you, you have peace beyond understanding. In the midst of heaviness and discouragement, you have joy unspeakable. In troubled times, you have every comfort and consolation. While the world wonders what will happen next, you have hope in your heart. Your heart has been toward the Lord, and His heart has been toward you. You have taken care of the things that concern Him, and He has taken care of the things that concern you. You have given Him all that is yours, and He has given you all that is His.

Your plans are now His purposes. Your commitments are based on His leading. Your desires fit into His design.

You have sought His highest, and He has given you His best.

You are a chosen generation, a royal priesthood,
a holy nation, His own special people, that you may
proclaim the praises of Him who called you
out of darkness into His marvelous light.

1 PETER 2:9

ANOINTING AND TALENT

When someone sings and you are caught up with the beauty of her voice, that is talent. When someone sings and you are caught up with the beauty of the Lord, that is anointing.

When someone speaks and gets you to follow him, that is talent. When someone speaks and gets you to follow Jesus, that is anointing.

When someone counsels you and builds your confidence, that is talent. When someone counsels you and builds your faith, that is anointing.

When you are filled with self-confidence and achieve your goals, that is talent. When you are filled with the Holy Spirit and do the will of God, that is anointing.

When you work hard and receive human applause, that is talent. When you remain faithful and receive the approval of God, that is anointing.

He who establishes us with you in Christ
and has anointed us is God.

2 CORINTHIANS 1:21

HIS KINGDOM WITHIN YOU

The scribes and Pharisees who lived during the years of Jesus's ministry were a group of outwardly religious people who tried to establish their righteousness through works and by keeping rules and traditions. They worked hard at it, but it did not produce any joy or peace within them. Instead, they were without faith, hard, demanding, angry, critical, and judgmental. Their outward form of righteousness left them empty. And when they were confronted with the reality of the kingdom of God through Jesus Christ, they became more miserable.

We cannot walk in daily peace and joy if we carry unrighteousness in our hearts. The unrighteousness of bitterness, resentment, and unforgiveness will rob us of our peace and joy. The unrighteousness of worry, fear, and anxiety will stop the flow of the Holy Spirit within us. Everything about righteousness is good, pure, clean, wholesome, and healthy to us. Attitudes of unrighteousness will hinder the peace and joy of the Holy Spirit, but righteousness will release them. The fruit of righteousness is not sour grapes.

> *The kingdom of God is not eating and drinking,*
> *but righteousness and peace and joy in the Holy Spirit.*
>
> Romans 14:17

RESCUED

A riptide is a strong surface flow of water returning seaward from the shore. It can be extremely dangerous, dragging people away from the beach and leading to possible death as they attempt to fight the current and become exhausted. Hundreds of people are rescued from riptides each year.

There are spiritual riptides that can be a danger to our walk with Jesus Christ. Sometimes they can be subtle, but once we are in their grip, they can pull us away from our peace, our joy, and our trust in the Lord.

Riptides are stronger when the surf is rough as the result of a storm. When we go through rough times and difficult circumstances, the pull of the enemy can be the strongest. He can attack our minds with fear, anxiety, doubt, and worry. These thoughts can work like riptides as they try to drag us into the deep waters of discouragement, depression, or despair. Thankfully, God is like our lifeguard, rescuing us and bringing us back to safety.

[The LORD] rescued us from our enemies,
for His mercy endures forever.

PSALM 136:24

WHEN THE ANSWER IS NO

It's good to have technology in our cars. A smart car won't let you lock the doors if you don't take the key out of the ignition. It's nice to have a car that's smart enough to keep you from doing something that dumb! In a way, a smart car refuses to answer your request because it knows that if it did, you would be in a difficult situation.

When we come to God with certain petitions, we can be eternally grateful that sometimes His answer is "no." It is important for us to understand that His "no" is not based upon our lack of sincerity, but upon the greatness of His wisdom. He is too wise to say yes to any prayer that would bring us more harm than good if it were granted.

This is the confidence that we have in Him,
that if we ask anything according to His will, He hears us.

1 John 5:14

OUR RESPONSE TO GOD

The psalmist tells us to serve the Lord with gladness. His praise shall continually be in our mouths. God is always worthy of praise. Nothing about Him changes. Even during our most difficult days He is still faithful, still true, still on the throne, and still working out His plan.

God never promised us an easy life or one free of trials, hardships, or suffering. These things should not surprise us if we are following His ways. We know Jesus learned obedience by the things He suffered, and for the joy set before Him, He endured the cross. The apostle Paul went through great difficulties, yet he said he would gladly suffer the loss of all things to gain Christ (Philippians 3:8).

In this you greatly rejoice, though now for a little while,
if need be, you have been grieved by various trials.

1 Peter 1:6

THE GIFT OF ENCOURAGEMENT

Here's how to identify someone who needs encouragement," goes the old saying: "That person is breathing." Especially in today's age of cynicism and instant Internet criticism, encouragement matters more than ever.

The Scriptures describe God as one "who encourages those who are discouraged" (2 Corinthians 7:6 NLT). During a difficult time in his ministry, the apostle Paul found much-needed strength when the Lord Himself appeared to him, saying, "Be encouraged, Paul" (Acts 23:11 NLT).

Yes, apostles and prophets need encouragement, just like the rest of us. And those who receive encouragement are changed by it. Encouragement helps us muster the courage we might otherwise lack: the courage to face the day, to do what's right, to make a difference.

What inspires and encourages you? A hand-written note or card? A clever text message? A surprise phone call? An invitation to lunch or coffee? A personalized gift basket? Gestures like these can do so much to bless others—and you as well.

Pleasant words are a honeycomb,
Sweet to the soul and healing to the bones.

PROVERBS 16:24 NASB

WITNESSING WISDOM

Have you ever heard a joke you just didn't *get*? If you asked the joke teller for an explanation, chances are that the explanation did not suddenly make the joke funny.

As Christian women, we want to influence our friends, family, and coworkers who don't share our faith. Thus, we collect evidence, counterarguments, Bible verses, and all kinds of other tools to unleash the next time the opportunity arises. Unfortunately, you can win a debate about God and lose a chance to draw someone to Him.

Faith is often more about the will than the intellect. Jesus didn't say, "I will out-debate everyone so they will have no choice but to believe in Me." He said, "I will *draw* everyone to Me."

A war of words is unlikely to draw someone to faith. Or to spark a major change in one's life. But we can each do our part to bring others to our Savior. Love one another. Forgive one another. Be humble. Be insightful. Be a peacemaker. That kind of living has a way of drawing people in the right direction.

Be kind to one another, compassionate,
forgiving each other, just as God
in Christ also has forgiven you.

EPHESIANS 4:32 NASB

ALL IS YOURS

Jesus died and rose for you. This one truth is enough to radically transform our lives.

This is the taproot from which the tree of life grows, the headwaters from which the healing river flows, the pen from which all doctrine is written.

Justification, sanctification, redemption, and all the other truths of Scripture become yours because Jesus died and rose for you. "All the promises of God in Him are Yes" (2 Corinthians 1:20). Your life in Him is now an all-encompassing yes because Jesus died and rose for you. Hope is yours, life is yours, heaven is yours, and blessings upon blessings are yours, because Jesus died and rose for you.

All things are yours: whether…the world or life or death,
or things present or things to come—all are yours.
And you are Christ's, and Christ is God's.

1 Corinthians 3:21-23

NEW LIFE

When Jesus comes to live within us, He brings brand-new life, like springtime to our hearts—the cold, dark places in us are replaced with His glorious warmth and light, and the barren places with His fruitfulness.

New things come alive in us. The warming wind of His Spirit makes us feel fresh and clean. Seeds of faith are planted in the rich soil of His promises. Blossoms of hope begin to shoot forth. Young fruit trees begin to flow with the sap of His character and ministry.

Springtime in our hearts beckons us to grow—the seeds of faith need to be established, the blossoms of hope need to flower, and the fruit trees of His grace need to come to fruition. This new life leads us on—from faith to faith, from grace to grace, from glory to glory.

> *If anyone is in Christ, he is a new creation; old things*
> *have passed away; behold, all things have become new.*
>
> 2 CORINTHIANS 5:17

THE GIFT WE GIVE TO GOD

To be instantly healed from leprosy was amazing. It meant everything—a place in society, a job, hugs and human affection, belonging, acceptance, purpose, value. But what is even more amazing is that only one out of the ten was grateful enough to return and to pour out his thanks to Jesus.

The apostle Paul wrote to young Timothy, "In the last days… people will be…ungrateful" (2 Timothy 3:1-2 NIV). We live in an ungrateful world. To listen to most, you would think either God didn't exist, or if He did, He was indifferent, unkind, and uncaring.

God's generosity to us in Jesus Christ is overwhelming—God gives us a clean heart, a joyful heart, a loving heart, a peaceful heart—yet, there is one thing God cannot give us, and that is a thankful heart. Thankfulness is our gift to Him.

As He entered a certain village, there met Him ten men
who were lepers, who stood afar off. And they lifted up their
voices and said, "Jesus, Master, have mercy on us!"…
And one of them, when he saw that he was healed,
returned, and with a loud voice glorified God.

Luke 17:12-15

THE COMFORT
OF HIS PRESENCE

When God's people go through great hardships and heartaches, we often wonder what we can say to bring true comfort and hope. We can start by affirming that God is there, in the midst of it all, drawing closer than any friend or family member ever could. Jesus didn't isolate from us, hiding from our sorrows in heaven—He ministered to us and worshipped with us.

In the book of Revelation, God reaches out to those who have endured great tribulation and spreads His tabernacle over them—the tabernacle of His presence to protect them. In the midst of our deepest sorrows, tears, and struggles, God spreads the tent of His presence over us!

I heard a loud voice from heaven saying,
"Behold, the tabernacle of God is with men,
and He will dwell with them, and they shall be His people.
God Himself will be with them and be their God."

Revelation 21:3

THERE'S NO PLACE LIKE HOME

Here are six characteristics of the home Jesus wants to establish within us.

A home of love, where His arms are extended to help, to support, to encourage, and to embrace.

A home of acceptance, where we are valued, celebrated, enjoyed, and appreciated.

A home of protection, where we can be sheltered from the battering winds that beat against our lives.

A home of fellowship, where we can open our hearts, express our feelings, and share our thoughts.

A home of light, where we can find our way and fully discover the treasures within.

A home of warmth, where the fire of His presence burns bright. Its beauty draws us close, and the golden flames of mercy and grace warm the deepest chills.

> *Anyone who loves me will obey my teaching.*
> *My Father will love them, and we will come to them*
> *and make our home with them.*
>
> JOHN 14:23 NIV

WILL THE REAL YOU PLEASE STAND UP!

You are the Lord's, wholly and completely. There are no doubts in His mind. The devil has no lien against your life. Because of the price Jesus paid on the cross, Satan has no rightful claim upon you. He cannot approach the courts of heaven and say, "The shed blood of Jesus Christ was not payment enough to claim this life. I am owed back payment, and I refuse to release my legal rights."

Satan also has no parental right over you. The devil is not your father, and he cannot say, "This is my child, and I have every right to my authority over him." You are God's child. You have been adopted into God's family. He is your Father, and you are a joint-heir with Jesus Christ. In Jesus, there are no ties to your past to pull you back, no fears to hold you back, and no chains to keep you back.

Fear not, for I have redeemed you;
I have called you by your name; you are Mine.

Isaiah 43:1

MINISTRY READINESS

We don't have a ministry because we decide to have one; we have a ministry because God gives us one. Our calling, our work, and the fruit that comes from them are God's doing, not ours. Our privilege is to obey what God tells us to do. Our responsibility is to serve Him faithfully, whether our work is done in private or in public. His blessing and His anointing come to us when we live according to His will.

We cannot manufacture God's blessing and anointing simply by being ambitious, highly motivated, or hardworking. God's anointing and blessing come through the work of the Holy Spirit, not our own efforts. An ounce of obedience is worth more than a pound of strife and a ton of effort.

Paul, a bondservant of Jesus Christ, called to be
an apostle, separated to the gospel of God.

ROMANS 1:1

PUNCTUATION MARKS

Exclamation points have been called "screamers" or "gaspers." We often find this piece of punctuation at the end of sentences that evoke panic or fear.

God has not given us the spirit of fear; He has promised to give us peace. He doesn't want to frighten us, nor does He want to take away our hope. As He helps us write our life stories, God uses lots of commas. A comma signifies a brief pause. It lets you know that after the pause, something else will follow. God wants you to know there is something ahead that He has planned for you. Let's not put periods or exclamation points where God wants a comma.

Do not remember the former things, nor consider
the things of old. Behold, I will do a new thing,
now it shall spring forth; shall you not know it?
I will even make a road in the wilderness
and rivers in the desert.

Isaiah 43:18-19

KEEP YOUR HEART FULL OF HOPE

God wants us to keep our hope in Him and not in this world's system or its leaders. We are in this world, but not of it. God placed us here for an eternal purpose—to be a light of hope that needs to be seen, to be a voice of truth that needs to be heard, to be a demonstration of love that needs to be shared.

Humanity's plans will fail, but God's plan will prevail. His kingdom will come. His truth will endure. The change God brings will be everlasting—the world will pass away, sin will be no more, death will be overcome, the devil and all his demons will be cast into hell, Jesus will reign in righteousness, and there will be a new heaven and earth filled with His glorious light. This is our true hope.

The kingdoms of this world have become
the kingdoms of our Lord and of His Christ,
and He shall reign forever and ever!

REVELATION 11:15

YOUR VALUE

At auctions, people bid on items they value. Each item purchased is worth whatever someone is willing to pay—the greater the value, the greater the price.

One of the things that will increase the value of an item is its rarity. If there are one hundred of an item, it has some value. If there are only ten of that same item, it has greater value. But if there is only one of that item in existence, it has the greatest value of all.

Have you ever wondered what your true value is? If your life were up for auction, what would you be worth? When Jesus went to the cross, He paid the highest price for your life. To God, you are worth the death of His Son. Why such a high price? There are not one hundred of you; there are not ten of you. There is only one of you. To God, you are irreplaceable. That is why Jesus came to seek and to save you. He was not willing that you should perish. You are the lost sheep that needed to be found.

Christ died for us.

Romans 5:8

LOOKING UP, LOOKING DOWN

As important as it is for us to look up every day, it is equally important to look down.

Through our spiritual eyes, God provides two distinct views of faith. You can keep looking up because you are on a pilgrim's journey here on earth. You can keep looking down because you are seated with Christ in heavenly places: a place of rest, a place of triumph, a place of power, a place of authority, and a place of glory. His place is your place, His victory is your victory, and His life is your life. You can keep looking down because He has conquered the grave, because the enemy is below His feet, and because you are more than a conqueror through Him who loves you.

God raised us up with Christ and seated us with him
in the heavenly realms in Christ Jesus.

Ephesians 2:6 niv

DIVINE COMFORT

God's comfort is truly amazing. Think of a mother coming to the aid of her frightened child. A mother comforts her child by taking that child in her arms and holding it close to her heart. She speaks soft, soothing words to reassure her child that Mom is near and all will be well once again.

Like that child, we need God's comfort. Have you felt His arms lift you and draw you close to His heart? Have you heard His voice saying, "Peace, be still"?

> *All praise to God, the Father of our Lord Jesus Christ.*
> *God is our merciful Father and the source of all comfort.*
> *He comforts us in all our troubles.*
>
> 2 CORINTHIANS 1:3-4 NLT

REAL GRACE
FOR REAL PEOPLE

For many people, life is nothing more than playing a role. They act their way through life, trying to gain the approval and acceptance of others. They are bound by the fear of being exposed for who they really are, so they perform, seeking applause and recognition. Many Christians live this way, trying to impress others by acting out a spiritual role.

The life of Jesus brings us into reality, not role playing. To live in His reality, we must be real with Him. He wants us to come to Him as we are. He knows everything about us. We don't need to win Him over with a good performance. We should come to Him in sincerity and truth, in humility and brokenness, and in openness and honesty. When we do, He will not cast us out. He does not meet us with judgment but with mercy; He does not extend condemnation but grace.

The grace of our Lord Jesus Christ be with you all.

2 Thessalonians 3:18 kjv

WAITING

God doesn't always answer our prayers immediately. He fulfills His promises on His timetable, not ours. Why does God sometimes delay, and what does He want us to learn while we are waiting?

Perhaps God's answer is, "In times of waiting I want you to learn to stay steady and attentive to what I am saying. I want you to develop a hope that will keep you moving forward in My will until the end of your journey. Above all, I want you to add to your faith the benefit of patience, which will allow you to wait without complaint, and with a calm willingness to receive what I have for you, in the time frame that fits perfectly into My plan for your life."

We desire that each one of you show the same
diligence to the full assurance of hope until the end,
that you do not become sluggish, but imitate those
who through faith and patience inherit the promises.

Hebrews 6:11-12

JESUS, OUR
ONLY OPTION

From God's point of view, Jesus is not a good option or the best option—He's the *only* option. Without Jesus we have nothing and we can do nothing. With Him we have all things. All that God wants for us is found in Jesus Christ.

The best decision anyone can make is to give all to Jesus Christ. As we give our all, for His all, we find fulfillment.

Our decision to know and follow God is so important that He has presented us with only one option. Every road sign God has made points to one Person. Every message God has spoken proclaims one Name. Every view God shows us of Himself reveals one Face.

For us there is one God, the Father, of whom are all things,
and we for Him; and one Lord Jesus Christ, through whom
are all things, and through whom we live.

1 CORINTHIANS 8:6

WHAT'S IN YOUR BASKET?

Often, what the Holy Spirit deposits in your basket is a mystery. We do not know exactly what God has in mind for us, but we know God wants us to be sensitive to the leading of the Holy Spirit and to respond in simple faith and obedience.

As you go through your day, you may discover that the Holy Spirit has deposited within your basket a prayer He wants you to pray, a word of encouragement He wants you to speak, a blessing He wants you to give, or an act of kindness He wants you to extend.

We are God's handiwork, created in Christ Jesus to do good works, which God prepared in advance for us to do.

EPHESIANS 2:10 NIV

WITH AND WITHOUT

Being without certain things can be frustrating. Being without the important things in life can be devastating. No one wants to live without the love and care of family, the companionship of good friends, the warmth of home, the availability of food, or the supply of clean drinking water.

By far, the worst imaginable thing is to be without God. To live without God is to live without discovering why you were made. To live without God is to be without hope, to be without light.

To be without God means you can have it all and still be empty. You can fill your life with pleasures and entertainment and still be without joy. You can protect yourself with every possible security and still lack peace. You can receive every type of reward and recognition and still be searching for meaning and purpose. But with God, you can enjoy a full life, no matter what you might be lacking. Indeed, the presence of God is more important than the absence of anything else.

> *[Teach] them to observe all things that I have*
> *commanded you; and lo, I am with you always,*
> *even to the end of the age.*
>
> Matthew 28:20

THE PILGRIM'S JOURNEY

Many years ago a popular band recorded the song "I Still Haven't Found What I'm Looking For."

Christ's pilgrim is not someone who is wandering aimlessly in their search for meaning or purpose in life, but someone who knows what they are looking for. Christ's pilgrim is on a journey from earth to heaven, and on the journey the pilgrim never walks alone or wanders about without a purpose.

The Bible tells us to seek the Lord, and that if we seek Him we will find Him. The pilgrim whom the Bible addresses in 1 Peter is not someone who is walking about trying to find God, but someone who walks with God, who knows God, and is being guided by God in every step she takes. The pilgrim is not looking for her place in this world because she has already found her place in Christ. The pilgrim's purpose is Christ; the pilgrim's destiny is Christ; the pilgrim's progress is Christ. For the pilgrim, life is not about the journey, but about Christ, the Author of the journey.

Seek first the kingdom of God and His righteousness,
and all these things shall be added to you.

MATTHEW 6:33

YOU ARE THE LORD'S

I t is no accident that you are alive today. God has made no mistakes concerning you. He has given you all the light you need to know His will, and all the grace you need to do His will. He knows everything about you—your ups and downs, your highs and lows. He knows your thoughts, He knows your heart, and He is acquainted with all your ways.

He has laid His hand of blessing upon you, and has placed His covering over you. He knows you by name and calls you His own. No one knows you better or loves you more. Today, you are in God's place, in God's time, to fulfill God's plan, in God's way, by God's grace, for God's glory.

> *My frame was not hidden from you when I was made*
> *in the secret place... Your eyes saw my unformed body;*
> *all the days ordained for me were written in your book...*
> *How precious to me are your thoughts, God! How vast is the*
> *sum of them! Were I to count them, they would outnumber*
> *the grains of sand—when I awake, I am still with you.*
>
> PSALM 139:15-18 NIV

SECURE AND CERTAIN

We are living in times of great uncertainty. The Bible makes it clear there is only one thing that cannot be shaken: the kingdom of God. Everything about His kingdom is solid, unmovable, unshakeable, incorruptible, and undefiled. The wise woman builds her life on Jesus Christ, on the truth of His words, and on the reality of His kingdom.

In our uncertain times, God wants us to live as people of faith and not people of sight. We are to be people who live amid fear, yet have peace; people who live amid sorrow, yet have joy; people who live amid trouble, yet have comfort; people who live amid uncertainty, yet have hope.

Know this, that in the last days perilous times will come.

2 Timothy 3:1

HIS PLAN FOR HIS GLORY

God has a plan and a purpose for everything He has made. Everything is for His glory. All things were made by Him and for Him, and He is working all things out according to the council of His own will. He doesn't need a consulting firm to give Him tips, He doesn't need university professors to give Him guidance, and He doesn't need religious leaders to give Him counsel.

God has a plan for His people, the body of Christ. He has a plan for the nations, and He has a plan for your life. God is working out His plan. Nothing can stop His plan or frustrate His purposes. God is not worried about what will happen or what He will be able to do. Nothing takes Him by surprise. He sees the future, and He is already there. He knows where He is leading your life, and He knows how to get you there in His perfect time and way.

[There is] one God and Father of all,
who is above all, and through all, and in you all.

Ephesians 4:6 kjv

DESTINY OR
THE WILL OF GOD?

What does it mean to fulfill our destiny? Some define destiny as our future place in heaven. Others define destiny as discovering our present purpose on earth. It is common to think of fulfilling our destiny as "reaching our full potential" or "being all that we can be." It is common to hear people say, "We must dare to dream big and accomplish our goals." This sounds noble, but it can be misleading and bring frustration and disappointment into people's lives as they pursue self-fulfillment.

The word "destiny" can evoke highly challenging, motivating, and inspiring thoughts in people's minds. It can also create delusions of grandeur. Many want to do big things for God, but not too many want to do the little things or the unnoticed things. It is easy to assume that if people fulfill their destiny they will become important, popular, or influential. God's destiny for us includes doing His work here on earth. That work is important to Him, regardless of whether or not the rest of the world takes notice. We do our best work when we do it for an audience of One.

*For us there is one God, the Father, of whom are all things,
and we for Him; and one Lord Jesus Christ, through whom
are all things, and through whom we live.*

1 Corinthians 8:6

PEACE WITH GOD

Peace with God means you stand before Him in quietness and rest, knowing that everything between you and Him is all right. You were strangers, but now you are friends. You were an alien, but now you are a citizen of His kingdom. You were an outsider, but now you are part of His eternal family.

There are no walls between you and God, no fences dividing you, no gulfs separating you. Your back is no longer turned—you stand face-to-face in communion and fellowship. He is your Father, and you are His child.

Having been justified by faith, we have peace with God through our Lord Jesus Christ.

ROMANS 5:1

GOD IS FOR YOU

To say "I know so" is not the same as saying "I hope so," "I think so," or "I pray so." It means far more than recalling various facts or trivia. It means to be absolutely, positively convinced about something with all your mind, all your heart, and all your soul. It means to be so certain of something that you are willing to cast all your care, all your worry, all your fears, and your very life upon it.

Thankfully, as God's children, we don't have to guess His true thoughts toward us. One way the enemy can defeat us is to deceive us. He tells us lies, hoping we will believe them. He might tell you that God is against you. If you believe this lie, you will doubt God's love and care for you. Let's choose to believe the truth: God loves us unconditionally, and we can always place our complete trust in Him.

When I cry out to You,
then my enemies will turn back;
this I know, because God is for me.

PSALM 56:9

HOLY HUMILITY

To walk humbly before God, we must understand our dependency upon God. Many scriptures illustrate this dependency. We are told that He is the True Vine and we are the branches; He is the Potter and we are the clay; He is the Shepherd and we are the sheep; He is the Head and we are the body; He is the Giver and we are the receivers; He is the Master and we are His servants.

Without the Vine, the branch would shrivel. Without the Potter, the clay would lack form. Without a Shepherd, the sheep would be without care. Without the Head, the body would die. Without the Giver, we would be empty. Without a Master, we would be left to our own ways. These truths should keep us humble but also keep us grateful.

You younger people, submit yourselves to your elders.
Yes, all of you be submissive to one another,
and be clothed with humility, for "God resists
the proud, but gives grace to the humble."

1 Peter 5:5-6

TRIUMPH OVER TRIBULATION

Regardless of the times in which we live, we will face certain challenges, such as tribulation. This is nothing new. The church of Jesus Christ has been living through tribulation since its birth 2,000 years ago.

However, Jesus does not want us to focus on tribulation, but on Him. He has overcome the world, but if we focus on tribulation, the world can easily overcome us with worry, fear, and anxiety.

We should remember Jesus's assurance that even though we will face tribulation, we can have His perfect peace. He also encourages us to be of good cheer. Let's allow God's perfect peace and good cheer to influence our thinking, our speech, and our attitudes each day.

These things I have spoken to you, that in Me you may have peace. In the world you will have tribulation; but be of good cheer, I have overcome the world.

JOHN 16:33

GOD IS FAITHFUL

God does not want you to focus on your needs, but on His faithfulness; not on worldly problems, but on His faithfulness; not on circumstances, but on His faithfulness; not on your feelings or opinions, but on His faithfulness; not on political change, but on His faithfulness.

We all need to be reminded of God's faithfulness from time to time. Our feet need to stand upon His faithfulness. Our hearts need to trust in His faithfulness. Our emotions need to celebrate His faithfulness, and our mouths need to proclaim His faithfulness.

> *O Lord God of Heaven's Armies! Where is there anyone as mighty as you, O Lord? You are entirely faithful.*
>
> Psalm 89:8 nlt

MERCY, PEACE, LOVE

t's a new day. You have never gone this way before. What you have planned for today is not what makes it meaningful. It's meaningful because God is in it.

He was in it when you first opened your eyes. He has sustained you through the years and greeted you with new mercies at morning's light. He has given you the breath of life and promised to direct your steps until your journey is complete.

Because of God's mercies, you can follow Him with all of your heart today, assured that there is nothing being held over your head to condemn you. You can take each step with a quiet heart, knowing that His peace keeps you steady and sure. You can move ahead with great faith, knowing His love keeps you close to His heart, mindful of His promises, and confident of His care.

May God give you more and more mercy, peace, and love.

JUDE 1:2 NLT

GOD'S PROVISIONS
FOR TODAY

Are you tired or weary? Allow God to renew you with His strength.

Are you discouraged or downhearted? Allow God to lift you with His love.

Are you carrying a burden of sin? Allow God's mercies to restore you.

Do you need reassurance? Allow God to hold you in His embrace.

Do you need healing? Allow God to mend you with His touch.

You are His child, and He is your Father—you belong to Him, and He belongs to you. He matters to you, and you matter to Him. You are committed to Him, and He is committed to you. Today there is mercy, there is peace, and there is love.

I will abundantly bless her provision;
I will satisfy her poor with bread.

PSALM 132:15

STORMS OF LIFE

The size and strength of a tsunami are formidable. To see these waves move upon the land is staggering. The lesson is clear: When a tsunami is heading your way, don't run toward the beach to get a better view, or try clinging to a palm tree to wait out the storm. Run instead to the high ground—that's where you will find refuge.

In Psalm 61:2, King David said, "Lead me to the rock that is higher than I." David knew where to flee in times of danger. Like David, we must not think that we are smarter or stronger than life's storms. We cannot outrun them or outsmart them. Our enemies are too strong to be defeated by naive zeal or human determination. Let's be thankful that our victory over every storm of life can be found in the Lord.

You rule the raging of the sea;
when its waves rise, You still them.

PSALM 89:9

STABILITY IN YOUR LIFE

Uncertainty is everywhere. Things that seemed secure have become unstable. Foundations that seemed like rocks have turned into sand, and confidence has turned into confusion. Many people have looked for security and stability in places that seemed safe and secure, but these places are unable to bear the pressures of our times.

Only God can be our stability in an unstable world, our certainty in uncertain times. Only God knows what is ahead for us and where we are going. Only God can speak to us with the voice of certainty, assuring us, "This is the way, walk ye in it" (Isaiah 30:21 KJV).

> *Wisdom and knowledge will be the stability*
> *of your times, and the strength of salvation;*
> *the fear of the LORD is His treasure.*
>
> ISAIAH 33:6

HAVE JOY

Joy is a gift from God, not the result of a particular circumstance that happens in our lives. Joy touches our spirits; fun touches our emotions. Joy abides, while fun comes and goes. Joy flows like deeps waters, while fun skips along like a rock across the water's surface.

Joy is amazing and strength-giving. Joy isn't just for the good times, but for the hard times as well. Jesus focused on joy even while going through the agony and suffering of the cross. The joy Jesus knew is the joy we can experience as we face every circumstance of life—hard or easy, bad or good, pleasant or difficult. That's the kind of joy He offers to us.

May the God of hope fill you with all joy and peace
in believing, that you may abound in hope
by the power of the Holy Spirit.

ROMANS 15:13

HEAVEN, OUR HOME

The Bible mentions heaven many times, but it does not provide many details. First Corinthians 2:9-10 may explain why. Perhaps heaven and what God has ahead for us there is so overwhelmingly magnificent that God could only say, "If I painted it, your eye couldn't grasp it all. If I told it, your ears couldn't absorb it all. If I wrote it, your mind couldn't imagine it all."

Some people tend to minimize heaven. They think that life here on earth (based on what they have seen, heard, or imagined) is as good as it gets. Their concept of heaven is not exciting, but rather monotonous and boring. They know nothing of the language, the sounds, the sights, and the realities of heaven. Whatever heaven turns out to be, it will be better than anything that anyone has imagined.

> *"No eye has seen, no ear has heard, and no*
> *mind has imagined what God has prepared for*
> *those who love him." But it was to us that God*
> *revealed these things by his Spirit. For his Spirit*
> *searches out everything and shows us God's deep secrets.*
>
> 1 Corinthians 2:9-10 nlt

OUR GOD IN GRIEF

We live in a fallen world, and as a result, we all experience pain. Every one of us will likely experience the hurt of a relationship destroyed or of a loved one lost. Fortunately, God is Lord over all of it—the pain, the questions, the helpless feelings.

Our God knows when we are hurting, and He is there for us every second, through every teardrop. Someday, we will see His whole plan and how He loved us through every second, even the moments of heartbreak. *Especially* the moments of heartbreak.

For now, we can rest in the understanding that God's heart is good and His promises are true. He will fulfill His promise to work all things for our good if we love and serve Him. We know with absolute certainty that He will be our comforter and our deliverer in our times of pain and grief. And we can rest in the knowledge that we cannot go anywhere—even the depths of despair—where God cannot reach us.

Blessed are those who mourn,
for they will be comforted.

MATTHEW 5:4 NIV

YOU BELONG TO AN ETERNAL KINGDOM

We exist in a world that is temporary, but we live for the things that are eternal. Every human system or power will eventually falter, fail, and fade from view. Throughout history kings have been overthrown, leaders have fallen from power, kingdoms have been conquered, armies have been defeated, riches have been depleted, and fortresses have been toppled.

There is no secure place around us where the insecure can find a haven. Only in the kingdom of God can anyone find true rest and security. No rebellion can overthrow God's kingdom, no weapon can penetrate its defenses, and no warrior can dethrone its King.

Everything about the kingdom of God is solid, sure, and steady. It is reliable, dependable, and impenetrable. The kingdom of God is eternal. It is the only kingdom that will remain. That's why God's kingdom is the only one we should embrace with our whole hearts.

Since we are receiving a Kingdom that is unshakable, let us be thankful and please God by worshiping him with holy fear and awe.

Hebrews 12:28 nlt

THE NEW COVENANT

When Jesus came, He came to save you, cleanse you, forgive you, and deliver you from your sins. He lived a sinless life so He could offer Himself upon the cross as your substitute. He was the sacrificial lamb who atoned for your sin.

The blood of Jesus cleanses you and claims you. He is your Redeemer, and He has taken full responsibility for your life. The shed blood of Jesus means your past is forgiven and your present and future are with Him. The loudest message of the new covenant is, "I love you, I have bought you, and you are Mine."

May the God of peace who brought up our Lord Jesus
from the dead, that great Shepherd of the sheep, through
the blood of the everlasting covenant, make you complete in
every good work to do His will, working in you what is
well pleasing in His sight, through Jesus Christ,
to whom be glory forever and ever. Amen.

HEBREWS 13:20-21

YOU HAVE ALL YOU NEED

The grace of God covers you, the presence of God is in you, the angels of God are with you, the arms of God are around you, the gifts of God are for you, and the power of God is upon you. He has not abandoned you or forsaken you.

He has called you and equipped you to serve Him. He has given you the ministry of reconciliation so you can reach out to others. He has given you the ministry of intercession so you can pray for others, and He has given you the ministry of hope so you can comfort others.

God is for you, the Holy Spirit is in you, and Jesus is with you. All the heavenly hosts are on your side. The weapons of your warfare are mighty through God to the pulling down of strongholds. He has given you the whole armor of God for every battle you face. He has you covered from head to toe.

Take unto you the whole armor of God,
that ye may be able to withstand in the evil day,
and having done all, to stand.

Ephesians 6:13 KJV

GOD WILL NOT FAIL YOU

The depth of God's love for us cannot be measured, and its height cannot be scaled. He wants you to trust Him completely because He will not fail you. He cannot. When you go through trials, He will keep you from defeat. When you face temptations, He will keep you from shame.

When the enemy comes in like a flood, He will raise up a standard against him. No weapon formed against you will prosper, for the battle is the Lord's. You will never face an enemy you have to fear or run from, for "greater is he that is in you, than he that is in the world" (1 John 4:4 KJV). Your life belongs to Him and your times are in His hands.

Let your conversation be without covetousness;
and be content with such things as ye have: for
he hath said, I will never leave thee, nor forsake thee.
So that we may boldly say, The Lord is my helper,
and I will not fear what man shall do unto me.

HEBREWS 13:5-6 KJV

GOD WILL NEVER LET YOU GO

Jesus is with you always. No one can pluck you out of His hand.

He is in you, and you are in Him. He is your Shepherd, and He will watch over you. You need not fear any evil. He is your High Priest. He intercedes for you daily, and His prayers are being answered. He is your Bridegroom. He is preparing a place for you in His Father's house and He will come for you.

He holds you with His pierced hands. If you ever question His love for you, look at His hands. His arms were once outstretched on the cross so He could embrace you now with His unfailing love.

When He shed His blood, He took your sin; when He died on the cross, He took your death; when He descended into hell, He took your judgment. When He rose from the grave, He gave you eternal life.

[God] delivered us from so great a death, and doth deliver:
in whom we trust that he will yet deliver us.

2 Corinthians 1:10 kjv

THE VOICE OF THE LORD

God speaks. His voice is as loud as thunder and as soft as a whisper. His voice is recognizable to His children and as clear as a pure mountain stream. His voice is as soothing as the words of a mother speaking comfort to her hurting child, as assuring as the words of a father speaking courage to a fearful child.

God's voice is like no other. It is a peaceful voice, a healing voice, a seeking voice, a merciful voice, a majestic voice, a calling voice, an affirming voice, a great voice. We need to seek His voice, listen to His voice, respond to His voice, follow His voice, and trust His voice.

We do not need to avoid or fear God's voice. Everything He has to say to us is true, good, loving, and life-giving.

> *His feet [were] like unto fine brass, as if they burned in a furnace; and his voice as the sound of many waters.*
>
> REVELATION 1:15 KJV

GOD'S BLESSINGS
THROUGH HIS RICHES

As you walk with Jesus day by day, you will find that your thankfulness to Him is an ever-increasing symphony of praise, building into a lifelong crescendo of gratitude that flows from your heart to His. You, who have so little, have received so much because He has been so generous.

There are so many riches He has given to you, so many answers to prayer He has granted to you, so many kindnesses He has manifested to you, so many joys He has provided for you, so many mercies He has extended to you, so many blessings He has showered upon you. Everything you have has come from Him, and that is the reason why your heart can be so grateful.

Oh, how great are God's riches and wisdom
and knowledge! How impossible it is for us to
understand his decisions and his ways!

ROMANS 11:33 NLT

THE SCHOOL
OF THE HOLY SPIRIT

The moment you gave your life to Christ, He enrolled you in His school. Your teacher is the Holy Spirit, and life is your classroom. He has surrounded you with lots of fellow students, but you will always have His personal and undivided attention. When Jesus enrolled you in His school, He placed you there for a lifetime. Heaven is your graduation. Until that day, you will be taught by the Holy Spirit and have new lessons to learn.

Today, in your circumstances, in your relationships, in your trials, in your pain, in your persecutions, Jesus has things for you to learn. The Holy Spirit is teaching and instructing you in His ways, His working, and in His wisdom. He is teaching you about the kingdom of God, about the heart of God, and about God's plans and purposes for your life.

The Holy Spirit—he will teach you everything
and will remind you of everything I have told you.

John 14:26 NLT

PUFFED UP OR BUILT UP?

The Scriptures present many contrasts. God's Word unites and divides. It separates light from darkness, truth from error, sin from righteousness, flesh from Spirit, the carnal mind from the spiritual mind, the old man from the new man, the world from the kingdom of God, life from death, idolatry from true worship, a believer from an unbeliever, and Christ from the devil.

First Corinthians 8:1 also makes a clear distinction between what puffs us up and what builds us up. The Holy Spirit always works through love, which builds us up and never puffs us up. The purpose of teaching, preaching, or ministering in the body of Christ is to build believers up in Christ through love, not puff them up in the flesh.

Now concerning things offered to idols: We know that we all have knowledge. Knowledge puffs up, but love edifies.

1 Corinthians 8:1

GOD WILL ALWAYS
MEET YOUR NEEDS

God's faithfulness has never depended on the faithfulness of His children. He is faithful even when we aren't. We lack courage—He doesn't. He has made a history out of working through people in spite of our weaknesses.

Consider the feeding of the five thousand. It's the only miracle, aside from those of the final week, recorded in all four Gospels. Why did all four writers think it was worth repeating? Perhaps they wanted to show how God doesn't give up even when His people do.

When the disciples failed to pray, Jesus prayed. When the disciples didn't seek God, Jesus sought God. When the disciples were weak, Jesus was strong. When the disciples lacked faith, Jesus had faith.

God is greater than our weakness, and our weakness reveals how great God is. Let's be thankful that God is faithful even when His children are not.

My God shall supply all your need
according to His riches in glory by Christ Jesus.

Philippians 4:19

WAITING FOR GOD'S TIME

One of the ancient meanings of the word "wait" is "to bind together by twisting." Binding cords together by hand takes time and patience. God, like a master weaver, does a creative work within us during the waiting times in our lives. During our waiting times, God binds our lives with His, as a rope maker binds threads of twine. When this happens, we experience the stretching of our faith and the testing of our patience.

As He works, He strengthens us and pulls us closer to His heart. He does this because He desires intimacy with us. Before He gives us what we are waiting for, He wants to give us more of Himself. In the waiting times we are strengthened with His strength, and the fiber of His character is worked within us.

Rest in the LORD, and wait patiently for Him;
do not fret because of him who prospers in his way,
because of the man who brings wicked schemes to pass.

PSALM 37:7

THE FULLNESS
OF GOD'S GLORY

What is glory? In Hebrew it means splendor, honor, beauty, majesty, grandeur, or excellence. In Greek it means dignity, honor, praise, or esteem. No amount of words, however descriptive they may be, can help us fully grasp what glory truly is. Glory is not about what we describe—it's about what we behold.

Jesus Christ came so you could behold His glory. Not just a glimpse of His glory, but the fullness of His glory. As we grow in our relationship with Jesus Christ, we go from glory to glory. We see more of His beauty, learn more of His ways, and understand more of His heart. In many ways, we are like people watching sunbeams coming through the window of our heart—the sunbeams are real and delightful to look upon—but they are nothing compared to the full glory of the sun from which they emanate.

Now unto him that is able to keep you from
falling, and to present you faultless before
the presence of his glory with exceeding joy.

JUDE 1:24 KJV

NO ONE LIKE JESUS

Jesus lived like no man has ever lived. His obedience was clothed with joy, His motives were bathed in love, and His choices were covered with grace. Jesus spoke as no man had ever spoken. He spoke with authority. His words went deeper than the mind. They reached the soul, pierced the heart, touched the conscience, and stirred the spirit. Every heart that trusted what He said was changed forever.

Jesus worked as no man had ever worked. When He found the sick, He showed them the way to healing. When He found the impure, He showed them the way to cleansing. When He found the broken, He showed them the way to wholeness. When He found the heavy of heart, He led them to the fountains of joy. When He found those in darkness, He led them to His marvelous light. And when He found the thirsty, He led them to rivers of life.

> *Then they said to the woman, "Now we believe, not because of what you said, for we ourselves have heard Him and we know that this is indeed the Christ, the Savior of the world."*
>
> JOHN 4:42

NEVER LOSE SIGHT
OF ETERNITY

Your life will not end with a death certificate. God has made that null and void. There's true life ahead, at a deeper and more beautiful level than anything you can possibly experience in this world.

Life on earth is just the beginning. It's like the childhood of your eternity. Today is your chance to grow and learn, to get acquainted with God and His creations, to get a small, inviting taste of what's to come.

Embrace today with your whole heart. Enjoy it. Explore it. Give yourself fully to living it well. But never lose sight of eternity. There's so much more to real life than what you can see right now.

When you draw near to God, things in life will appear small compared to the realities of eternity.

This is eternal life: that people know you, the only true God, and that they know Jesus Christ, the One you sent.

JOHN 17:3 NCV

SEEING THE WORLD THROUGH GOD'S EYES

Imagine seeing the world through God's eyes. How would you feel about the woman in the wheelchair at the grocery store? The neighbor kid who's just found out his folks are getting a divorce? The homeless guy on the park bench?

Seeing individuals the way God does makes you want to put love into action and help. That's compassion kicking in. Compassion doesn't just feel sorry for people. It strives to make a positive difference in their lives. So ask God to help you see through His eyes—then to show you how to help. Even if the only action you can take is to pray, your compassion can make a difference in the world.

Seeing the world through eyes of compassion, you can care for everyone as if they were the only person in the entire world. Let's view people through eyes of love and take actions that will make a difference in our world.

You, O Lord, are a God full of compassion, and gracious,
longsuffering and abundant in mercy and truth.

PSALM 86:15

KEEP SEARCHING
FOR WISDOM

Where will you find wisdom today? Will you seek it from God or from the world? As a thoughtful woman living in a society filled with temptations and distractions, you know that the world's brand of "wisdom" is everywhere and it is dangerous. You live in a world where it's all too easy to stray far from the ultimate source of wisdom: God's holy Word.

When you commit yourself to the daily study of God's Word—and when you live according to His commandments—you will become wise. Today and every day, study God's Word and live by it. When you do, you will accumulate a storehouse of wisdom that will enrich your own life, and the lives of your family members, your friends, and the world around you.

I will instruct you and show you the way to go;
with my eye on you, I will give counsel.

PSALM 32:8 CSB

ON PASSION
AND PURPOSE

What is your passion in life? What do you enjoy more than anything else in the world—the kind of thing you will never grow tired of? Maybe it's music, art, teaching others, or some type of creative writing. If you have found your passion, you know there is a sense of godly wonder about it.

Are you pursuing your passion? Are you participating in the activities and pursuits you truly love? What ignites your sense of wonder and challenges you to be everything God created you to be?

If much of your life is sheer drudgery, you might be missing your life's ultimate purpose. Think about it: If you took away the paycheck, would you still want to do the job you have now?

You deserve no less than God's best for your life. You deserve to experience a vibrant life, in perfect harmony with your God-given abilities and heart's desires. So don't let your life be a series of random events. Live it on purpose; live it with holy passion. You'll be happy you did.

I do not run like someone running aimlessly;
I do not fight like a boxer beating the air.

1 CORINTHIANS 9:26 NIV

THE QUICKSAND
OF BITTERNESS

Do you feel stuck in the quicksand of bitterness or regret? If so, it's time to free yourself. Yes, forgiveness is difficult, but the world holds few (if any) rewards for those who remain angrily focused upon the past.

As imperfect human beings, most of us are quick to anger, quick to blame, slow to forgive, and even slower to forget. Yet we know it's best to forgive others, just as we have been forgiven.

Do you harbor bitterness toward anyone, including yourself? If you do, then it's time to forgive and move on. Bitterness and regret are not part of God's plan for you, but God won't force you to forgive others. It's a job only you can finish, and the sooner you finish it, the better.

Hatred stirs up strife,
but love covers all sins.

PROVERBS 10:12

MAKING GOD'S PRIORITIES YOURS

Have you fervently asked God to help prioritize your life? Have you asked Him to help you do what must be done? If so, then you're continually inviting your Creator to reveal Himself in a variety of ways.

When you make God's priorities your priorities, you will receive God's abundance and peace. When you make God a full partner in every aspect of your life, He will lead you along the proper path—His path. When you allow God to reign over your heart, He will honor you with spiritual blessings too numerous to count.

As you plan for the day ahead, make God's will your ultimate priority and plan. When you do, every other priority will fall neatly into place.

Draw near to God, and he will draw near to you.

JAMES 4:8 CSB

GOD IS CALLING

The God of the entire universe longs to communicate with *you*! Let that truth sink in for a moment. It's amazing but true.

Many of us would consider it the opportunity of a lifetime to, just once, talk with a favorite recording artist, athlete, CEO, or movie star. Unfortunately, we don't always show the same zeal for communicating with God, who loves us, who is far more fascinating than any person we could ever encounter, and who longs to fellowship with us.

God created the universe and everything in it. He created us to have a relationship with Him, and the only way to have a relationship with anyone is to spend time with him or her. With God, this time can include prayer, meditation, reading the Bible or Christian books, listening to music, and worship.

The Lord of all creation is waiting to fellowship with you. Open your eyes; open your heart. God wants to communicate with you right now!

The Lord looks down from heaven on the
entire human race; he looks to see if anyone
is truly wise, if anyone seeks God.

Psalm 14:2 nlt

GETTING IT DONE NOW

The old saying is familiar and true: Actions speak louder than words. As believers, we must beware: Our actions should demonstrate the changes Christ can make in the lives of those who walk with Him.

God wants us to act in accordance with His will, and to respect His commandments. We should not merely hear the instructions of God; we should live by them. And it is never enough to wait idly while others do God's work here on earth; we too must act.

Doing God's work is a responsibility each of us must bear. When we do, our loving heavenly Father rewards our efforts with a bountiful harvest.

When you make a vow to God, don't delay fulfilling it, because he does not delight in fools. Fulfill what you vow.

Ecclesiastes 5:4 csb

A PRACTICAL CHRISTIAN

What is "real" Christianity? Think of it as an ongoing relationship—an all-encompassing relationship with God and His Son, Jesus. Everyone has a relationship with God. The important question is whether that relationship honors Him or ignores Him.

We live in a world that discourages heartfelt devotion and obedience to God. Everywhere we turn, we are confronted by a mind-numbing assortment of distractions. Yet even on our busiest days, God beckons us to slow down and consult Him. When we do, we can receive the peace and abundance only He can give.

The Christian lifestyle is not one of legalistic dos and don'ts. It is positive, attractive, and joyful. Today, choose to please and praise Him, and you will experience pure joy.

Pure and undefiled religion before God and the Father
is this: to visit orphans and widows in their trouble,
and to keep oneself unspotted from the world.

James 1:27

DEALING WITH DISAPPOINTMENT

What do you do with the inevitable disappointments life hands you? Many of us internalize them and let them creep into our hearts, where they fester and cause worry, pain, and despair. Others are wiser, sharing disappointments with a friend, a relative, a pastor, or a counselor.

Maybe you hesitate to share your disappointments with others. You might think, *I feel guilty about complaining about my problems when my best friend is dealing with so much.*

If you feel this way, give someone a chance. Remember how the Bible portrays God's people as interdependent parts of a body. We all need each other, and when one part suffers, the whole body can be compromised.

Every burden is lighter when you have someone to help you share it. That's why God has given us the gift of each other. We carry each other when needed so the whole body can carry on.

Yes, there are many parts, but only one body.
The eye can never say to the hand,
"I don't need you." The head can't say to the feet,
"I don't need you."

1 Corinthians 12:20-21 nlt

GOD'S LOVE
IS CONSTANT

A lot of us live with a hidden fear that God is angry at us. Perhaps a church service or television show convinced us that God has a whip behind His back and a paddle in His back pocket, and He's going to nail us when we've gone too far.

No concept could be further from the truth! God is very fond of us and wants to share His love with us. Our heavenly Father is filled with compassion. He hurts when His children hurt. Even when we're under pressure and feel like nothing is going right, He is waiting for us, to embrace us whether we succeed or fail.

He doesn't wrangle or force His way into anyone's heart. He comes into our hearts like a gentle lamb rather than a roaring lion.

Lord, you are kind and forgiving
and have great love for those who call to you.

PSALM 86:5 NCV

TRUST GOD'S PROMISES

What do you expect from the day ahead? Are you expecting God to do wonderful things, or are you living beneath a cloud of doubt? The familiar words of Psalm 118:24 remind us of a profound yet simple truth: "This is the day which the LORD hath made; we will rejoice and be glad in it" (KJV).

For Christians, every day begins and ends with God's Son and God's promises. When we accept Christ into our hearts, God promises us the opportunity for earthly peace and spiritual abundance. But more importantly, He promises us the priceless gift of eternal life.

As we face life's inevitable challenges, why not arm ourselves with the promises of God's Word? When we do, we can expect the best results, not only for the day ahead, but also for eternity.

You need endurance, so that after you have done God's will, you may receive what was promised.

HEBREWS 10:36 CSB

WHEN DOUBTS CREEP IN

I f you've never had any doubts about your faith, then you can stop reading this now. But if you've ever been plagued by doubts about your faith or about God, then please keep reading because this is for you.

Even some of the most faithful Christians are plagued by occasional bouts of discouragement and doubt. But even when we feel far from God, God is never far from us. He is always with us, always willing to calm the storms of life. God is always willing to replace our doubts with comfort and assurance.

When the enemy makes you doubt your faith, seek God's presence by establishing a deeper, more meaningful relationship with His Son. We are most vulnerable to piercing words of doubt when we distance ourselves from the fellowship Christ has called us into.

In the multitude of my anxieties within me,
your comforts delight my soul.

PSALM 94:19

LOVING OUR ENEMIES

Of all the Bible's commandments, perhaps none is tougher than "Love your enemies" (Matthew 5:44). Jesus was not asking us to tolerate them or to do them a few favors. No, Jesus said to *love* them. The neighbor who spreads hurtful rumors about you. The so-called friend who backstabs you. The ex who can't seem to let bygones be bygones.

Loving an enemy is a hard, often unpleasant task. That's why prayer is the first step in the process. Pray that you'll have the grace, the will, and the patience to show love. Pray that your enemy will accept your efforts and goodwill. You might also need to pray about your own bitterness. That way, even if your prayers don't change an enemy's ugly qualities, they will still change *you*.

As you pray for your enemies and try to bring peace to your relationships with them, you might come to realize that these people are no less attractive to God, or loved by Him, than you are. Further, as you experience what hard work it is to love unlovable people, you might appreciate anew God's love for you.

I tell you, love your enemies.
Help and give without expecting a return.
You'll never—I promise—regret it.
LUKE 6:35 MSG

KNOWING GOD'S WORD

As a believer, you have the potential to grow in your personal knowledge of the Lord every day. You can do so through prayer, worship, an openness to the Holy Spirit, and a careful study of God's holy Word.

The Word of God contains powerful prescriptions for everyday living. If you sincerely seek to walk with God, it's wise to thoughtfully study His teachings. The Bible should be your road map for every aspect of your life.

Do you want to establish a closer relationship with your heavenly Father? Then study His Word every day. The Bible is a priceless, one-of-a-kind gift from God. Let's treat it that way and read it that way.

As newborn babes, desire the pure milk of the word,
that you may grow thereby.

1 Peter 2:2

THE IMPORTANCE
OF PERSPECTIVE

Our lives are often anything but simple. Our days can become tornadoes of busy schedules, interpersonal conflicts, and to-do lists that never get done. There must be a simpler way to navigate our lives.

For followers of Jesus, one key is living to make a difference. To serve our Lord by loving those around us and making our world at least a bit better.

Am I making the most of the time God has provided me? Sometimes we need to hit the pause button to answer this question thoughtfully. We need to slow down and ask, *What are the things in my life that feed and inspire me? And what should I be doing to feed, inspire, and serve others?*

The answers to these questions give us perspective. Yes, some of the mundane tasks still need to be done, but perhaps there is a way to do them with kindness and creativity and patience. In a way that makes our heavenly Father smile.

> *And what does the LORD require of you?*
> *To act justly and to love mercy*
> *and to walk humbly with your God.*
>
> MICAH 6:8 NIV

PAYING ATTENTION TO GOD

Who is in charge of your life? Is it God or is it something else? Have you given Christ your heart, your soul, your talents, your time, and your testimony? Or are you giving Him little more than a few hours each Sunday morning?

In the book of Exodus, God warns that we should place no gods before Him. Yet all too often, we place the Lord second, third, or fourth to other things that we worship. When we unwittingly place possessions or relationships above our love for the Lord, we create problems for ourselves.

Does God rule your heart? Make certain that the honest answer to that question is a resounding yes. In the life of every sincere believer, God comes first. Remember, God loves all of us as if there were only one of us.

Where your treasure is, there your heart will be also.

Luke 12:34

BE PATIENT
AND TRUST GOD

As a busy woman in a fast-paced world, waiting quietly for God is often difficult. Why? Because we often seek to live according to our own timetables, not God's. In our better moments, we realize that patience is not only a virtue, but also a commandment from God.

As human beings, we are impatient and impulsive by nature. We know what we want, and we know exactly when we want it. But God knows better. He has created a world that unfolds according to His plans, not ours.

God instructs us to be patient in all things. We must be patient with our families, our friends, and everyone else. We must also be patient with God as He unfolds His plan for our lives. After all, think how patient God has been with us.

Trust in Him at all times, you people;
pour out your heart before Him;
God is a refuge for us.

PSALM 62:8

YOUR INNER LIGHT

Don't be so obsessed about people's opinion of you! Why do you care so much what other people think?" As kids, how many of us heard this parental rhetoric as we struggled to fit in with friends on the block or peers at school?

Indeed, well-adjusted people understand that their happiness does not depend on the opinions of others. They know happiness is an inside job. They trust their knowledge, insights, and instincts. Their God-given sense of purpose. They allow themselves to operate according to God's Spirit living within them, rather than being manipulated by outsiders.

If you tend to be a people-pleaser, try to stop looking outside yourself for validation and approval. In other words, don't let *them* define your happiness. Take care of yourself on the inside. Look to God, your Creator and your daily Guide. Let His inner light illuminate your life's path.

> *The Spirit of the Sovereign LORD is on me, because*
> *the LORD has anointed me to proclaim good news to*
> *the poor. He has sent me to bind up the brokenhearted,*
> *to proclaim freedom for the captives and release*
> *from darkness for the prisoners.*
>
> ISAIAH 61:1 NIV

LOVE ACCORDING TO GOD

As a woman and a Christ-follower, you know the profound love you hold in your heart for your family and friends. As a child of God, you can only imagine the infinite love your heavenly Father holds for you.

God made you in His image and gave you salvation through Jesus Christ. And now, because you are God's wondrous creation, a question presents itself: How will you respond to His love? Will you ignore it or embrace it? Will you return it or neglect it?

When you embrace God's love, your life's purpose is forever changed. God, in His infinite love and mercy, is waiting to embrace you with open arms. Accept His love today and forever.

This is My commandment,
that you love one another as I have loved you.

John 15:12

DEALING WITH GUILT

Have you ever felt the ground of conviction give way beneath your feet? The ledge crumbles, your eyes widen, and down you go. Now what do you do? When we fall, we can dismiss it. We can deny it. We can distort it. Or we can deal with it.

We keep no secrets from God. Confession is not telling God what we did. He already knows. Confession is a simple agreement with God that our acts were wrong. How can God heal what we deny? How can God grant us pardon when we won't admit our guilt?

Yes, we try to avoid guilt. But is guilt so bad? We feel guilty because we know right from wrong and aspire to be better than we are. That's what guilt is: a *healthy* regret for telling God one thing and doing another.

There is therefore now no condemnation to
those who are in Christ Jesus, who do not walk
according to the flesh, but according to the Spirit.

ROMANS 8:1

GETTING TO SOLUTIONS

Let's face the facts: Today will not be problem-free. In fact, life is often an exercise in problem-solving. The question is not whether you will encounter problems but how you will solve them.

When it comes to solving the problems of everyday living, we often know precisely what needs to be done, but we may be slow in doing it—especially if what needs to be done is difficult or uncomfortable. So we put off till tomorrow what should be done today.

Psalm 34:19 reminds us that the Lord solves problems for "people who do what is right" (NCV). Usually, doing "what is right" means doing the uncomfortable work of confronting our problems sooner rather than later. The good news is the sooner we confront our problems, the sooner they will be behind us.

People who do what is right may have many problems,
but the LORD will solve them all.

PSALM 34:19 NCV

PERSONAL WORSHIP

Worship. In thousands of years, we haven't worked out all the wrinkles. We still struggle for the right words in prayer. We still fumble over Scripture. We don't always know when to kneel or stand. At times, we don't know how to pray. Worship can be a daunting task.

That's why God gave us the Psalms—a praise book for God's people. The collection of hymns and petitions are connected by a common thread—a heart hungry for God. Some psalms are defiant. Others are reverent. Some are to be sung. Others are to be prayed. Some are intensely personal. Others are written as if the whole world could use them.

This variety should remind us that worship is personal. There is no secret formula. Each of us worships differently. But each should worship as God leads.

> *Come, let's worship him and bow down. Let's kneel before the LORD who made us, because he is our God and we are the people he takes care of, the sheep that he tends.*
>
> PSALM 95:6-7 NCV

GOD IS HERE FOR YOU

Because God is omnipresent, we can sense His presence whenever we quiet our souls and pray to Him. But sometimes, amid the incessant demands of everyday life, we turn our thoughts far from God. When we do, we suffer.

Do you set aside quiet moments each day to praise our heavenly Father? As a woman who has received the gift of God's grace, you should. Silence is a gift you give to yourself and to God.

Feel God's presence in every situation and in every circumstance. Know He is with you, in times of celebration or sorrow. He will never leave your side, even when He seems to be far away.

The familiar words of Psalm 46:10 remind us, "Be still, and know that I am God." When we do, we encounter the awesome presence of our loving Father, and we are comforted in the knowledge that God is not just near, He is *here*.

The LORD is with you when you are with him.
If you seek him, he will be found by you.

2 CHRONICLES 15:2 CSB

BEING SET
APART AND FREE

Do you ever wonder if Jesus smiles when His lost sheep come stumbling into the fold—looking up at the Shepherd as if to ask, "Can I come in? I don't deserve it, but is there room in Your kingdom for one more?" The Shepherd looks down at the sheep and says, "Come in. This is your home."

Just as those sheep are secure in the fold, you are secure in your salvation. No one can take it away from you.

The psalmist reminds us that we who have been redeemed should say so! (See Psalm 107:2.) Let's never forget how good it feels to be saved. Let the redeemed of the earth say so!

We all show the Lord's glory, and we are being changed to be like him. The change in us brings ever greater glory, which comes from the Lord, who is the Spirit.

2 CORINTHIANS 3:18 NCV

ANSWERING THE CALL

God is calling you to follow a specific path He has chosen for your life. Heeding this call is a great way to make the most of your talents and the opportunities to use them.

Have you heard God's call? Are you pursuing it with vigor? If so, you are both fortunate and wise. But if you haven't discovered God's plan for your life, keep searching and keep praying.

God has important work for you to do—work that no one else on earth can accomplish. God has placed you in a particular location, among particular people, with unique opportunities to serve. And He has given you all the tools you need to succeed.

I urge you who have been chosen by God
to live up to the life to which God called you.

EPHESIANS 4:1 NCV

LET GOD TRANSFORM YOUR LIFE

Think for a moment about the "old" you, the person you were before you invited the Lord to reign over your heart. Now, think about the "new" you, the person you have become since then.

Is there a difference between the "old" and the "new and improved" version? There should be! When you accepted Jesus as your personal Savior, your life was changed forever and made whole.

The Bible teaches that when we welcome Christ into our hearts, we become new creations through Him. Our challenge is to behave like new creations. When we do, God fills our hearts, blesses our endeavors, and transforms our lives forever.

For you died, and your life is hidden with Christ in God.

COLOSSIANS 3:3

ESTABLISH A GROWING RELATIONSHIP WITH JESUS

Who's the best friend this world has ever had? Jesus, of course. And when you form a life-changing relationship with Him, He will be your best friend as well.

Jesus has offered to share the gifts of everlasting life and everlasting love with the world and with you. If you make mistakes, He will stand by you. If you fall short of His commandments, He will still love you. If you feel lonely or worried, He can touch your heart and lift your spirits.

Jesus wants you to enjoy a happy, healthy, and abundant life. He wants you to walk with Him and to share His good news. And with a friend like Jesus behind you, you can do it. When you abide in Jesus and follow in His footsteps, your life will be transformed in new and wonderful ways!

Whoever keeps his word, truly in him the love of God is made complete. This is how we know we are in him: The one who says he remains in him should walk just as he walked.

1 John 2:5-6 csb

SHARING YOUR FAITH

Our personal testimonies are extremely important, but sometimes we are afraid to share our experiences. And that is unfortunate.

In his second letter to Timothy, Paul wrote, "God has not given us a spirit of...timidity" (1:7 NLT). Paul's meaning is clear: When sharing our beliefs, we must be courageous, forthright, and unashamed. We have God's infallible word on our side, and that can persuade anyone.

We live in a world that desperately needs the healing message of Christ Jesus. Every believer bears responsibility for sharing the good news of our Savior. You know how He has touched your heart, so help Him do the same for others.

Sanctify the Lord God in your hearts, and
always be ready to give a defense to everyone
who asks you a reason for the hope that is in you.

1 Peter 3:15

KEEPING YOUR WORD

God is committed to you. He won't bail on His promises or put you on "prayer waiting" because a more important request has come in. He will do what He says.

Before you make a commitment, whether to a relationship, a job, or even to volunteer to sell donuts at church on Sunday mornings, you need to weigh the cost. Ask yourself if your time, energy, resources, and talents will allow you to follow through on your promise. Ask God to help you make commitments that fit with His purpose and direction for your life.

Then, make one more commitment. Commit whatever you're doing to God. Through success, failure, struggles, and growth, allow Him to help you keep your word.

If a man makes a promise to the Lord or says he will
do something special, he must keep his promise.
He must do what he said.

Numbers 30:2 ncv

WE CHOOSE GOD'S WAY

Have you ever noticed how some people who don't know Christ can show character and wisdom in managing their lives and raising their children? Perhaps they seem blessed and at peace because they have stumbled upon God's ways.

And if He blesses those who unknowingly walk in His ways, how much more will He bless those who give their hearts to Him and long to exercise His principles?

When we choose His way, He blesses our land, meets our needs, keeps us from fear, and gives us peace. What more could we ask for? Do the choices you make build your confidence in Christ, or in your own abilities and wisdom? Let's not miss God's blessing by going our own way.

> *If you walk in My statutes and keep My commandments…*
> *I will give peace in the land.*
>
> LEVITICUS 26:3,6

OUR MOST IMPORTANT CHOICE

Eternal life is not an event that begins when you die. Eternal life begins when you invite Jesus into your heart right here on earth. So it's important to remember that God's plan for you is not limited to the ups and downs of everyday life. If you've allowed Jesus to reign over your heart, you've already begun your eternal journey.

As mere mortals, our vision for the future, like our lives here on earth, is limited. God's vision is not impaired by such limitations. His plans extend throughout eternity.

Let us praise the Creator for His priceless gift, and let's share the good news with all who cross our paths. We return our Father's love when we share that love with others. When we do, we are blessed on earth and throughout eternity.

Now is a great time to accept God's offer of abundant and eternal life. Why not accept His gift today? A lifetime of eternal love and fellowship awaits you.

This is the will of Him who sent Me,
that everyone who sees the Son and
believes in Him may have everlasting life;
and I will raise him up at the last day.

JOHN 6:40